Understanding the Human Body

Story by **Hubert Ben Kemoun**
Factual accounts by **Brigitte Dutrieux**
Game by **Catherine Pauwels**

BARRON'S

contents

Story

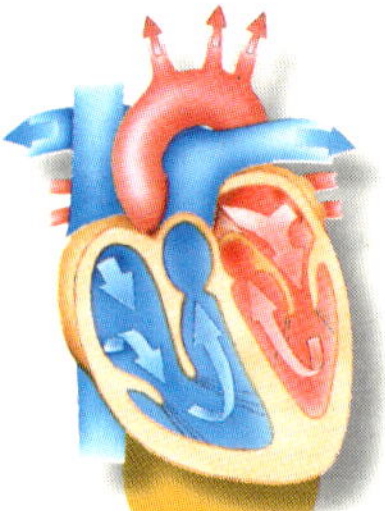

Mega-infos

Activity

Mega-infos

Game

Mega-infos

Anecdotes

Mega-infos

Activity

Mega-infos

Quiz

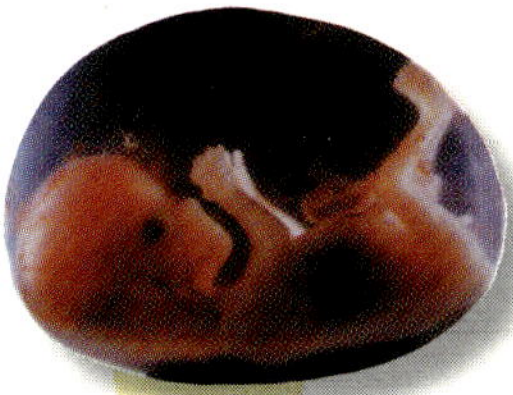

Stickers

Picture Cards

Story

On the Other Side

Hubert Ben Kemoun

The Crossing

The ferryboat's whistle startled a colony of seagulls that had gathered on the upper deck. Resting his elbows on the rail, Gregory watched them rise into the sky above the harbor entrance to Brick City. In spite of the strong wind and the spray it created, he had spent the entire crossing on deck. He hadn't wanted to miss any of the excitement of this adventure. Adventure? Just an hour's voyage on a ferryboat? But yes, adventure it was, because even though he was 13 years old, he had never taken a trip by himself before. And here he was, going to visit his penpal, Felicia.

Gregory would be spending two days with her and her family.

Felicia and her father were there waiting for him when he stepped off the boat. She had sent him photos of herself so he recognized her immediately. Her brown hair framed her face just the way it did in the pictures. Her eyes, however, were even greener and lovelier than the photos had shown. She ran up to Gregory and gave him a hug. He felt himself blush and hoped Mr. Griffon wouldn't notice.

"Welcome to Brick City, Gregory," said Mr. Griffon. "Did you enjoy the crossing?"

"Oh, yes, sir. It was great," replied Gregory as he took his place beside Felicia in the back seat of the car.

The harbor at Brick City was pretty much like the one at his hometown of Meckneb, on the other side of the bay. Huge cranes rose high above the docks, bordered by old warehouses. Felicia talked without stopping. She had planned lots of things to do. Visits to the downtown shopping mall, walks along the beach, swimming in the sea near her home. Gregory just listened, trying to smile and nod occasionally, but he found himself totally distracted by the hands that gripped the car's steering wheel. Mr. Griffon had twelve fingers! On each hand there were four fingers and two thumbs, one on each side of the

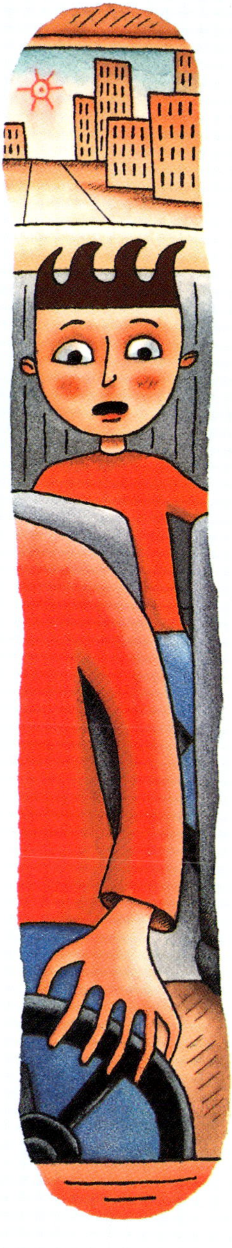

palm! By the time the car came to a stop in front of a large house that overlooked the sea, Gregory, without quite understanding why, had begun to feel very uncomfortable.

The Griffons' Home

Felicia, all smiles and chatter, showed Gregory the room that was to be his during his visit. She took his hand as they went back downstairs. Why did it feel so strange? He didn't dare look down. Only when they were outside and she pointed to a little island, was he unable to avoid looking at her hand. It was just like her father's—four fingers in the middle, two thumbs on either side!

"I'm so happy that you've come at last," Felicia was saying, her other hand on his arm. He could feel the pressure of the two thumbs and hoped she didn't notice the shudder that rippled through his body.

"So am I," lied Gregory.

"I really can't wait to get started."

Gregory just nodded.

"Felicia! Gregory! Lunch is ready." Mrs. Griffon was calling them from the back door of the house.

"Let's go!" said Felicia, reaching for Gregory's hand.

Pretending not to notice, Gregory raced ahead. "I really am hungry," he called back to Felicia.

"All that sea air, I guess," Felicia said, laughing.

"Well . . . so this is the famous Gregory that Felicia has talked about so much," exclaimed Mrs. Griffon when they got back to the house. She looked a lot like Felicia, with the same brown hair, green eyes, and yes . . . twelve fingers!

Gregory had thought that Felicia had inherited her strange hands from her father. But both parents! How could it be? Should he ask about it? No, of course he couldn't do that. It didn't seem to bother the Griffons at all. If he *were* to ask, it might embarrass them.

During lunch at the Griffons', no one in the family seemed to notice Gregory's discomfort. As they left the dining room, Felicia suggested that she and Gregory take a walk.

"Put your swimming trunks on under your jeans," she said. "Maybe we'll go for a swim."

On the narrow trail overlooking the sea it wasn't possible to walk side by side. Felicia, skipping briskly on the packed sand, went ahead. From time to time she turned to tell him about things they were seeing or to call his attention to places that she particularly liked. Gregory's heart felt heavy in his chest. He and Felicia had written to each other for almost two years, had seemed to have so much in common. She was his first . . . well, girlfriend. He had even had daydreams

about their possible future together. How little he had really known about her.

Just before they got to the beach, they met a fisherman returning home. As they moved aside to let him pass, Gregory couldn't keep from glancing at the old man's hands. Twelve fingers!

After Gregory and Felicia had spread their beach towels on the sand, Felicia pulled her tee shirt over her head. She had on a two-piece bathing suit. Oh no, thought Gregory, it can't be! Two navels!

"What's the matter?" asked Felicia, noticing the strange look on Gregory's face. "Aren't you going in the water?"

"Not just now," he answered. "Maybe a little later. You go ahead."

Some of Felicia's friends approached, with their ugly hands and double belly buttons. Gregory could hardly stand being introduced to them. Shaking hands with the other boys was torture. Felicia walked away with them, toward the water, turning and giving him a little wave with her hand. That awful fan-shaped hand!

Gregory looked around him at the sunbathers stretched out on their colorful beach towels. They all had the same grotesque hands—and, on all the bare stomachs he could see, there were two navels, side by side. Gregory began to feel dreadfully homesick.

And sick in other ways too. His stomach was doing flip-flops. Was he going to lose his lunch?

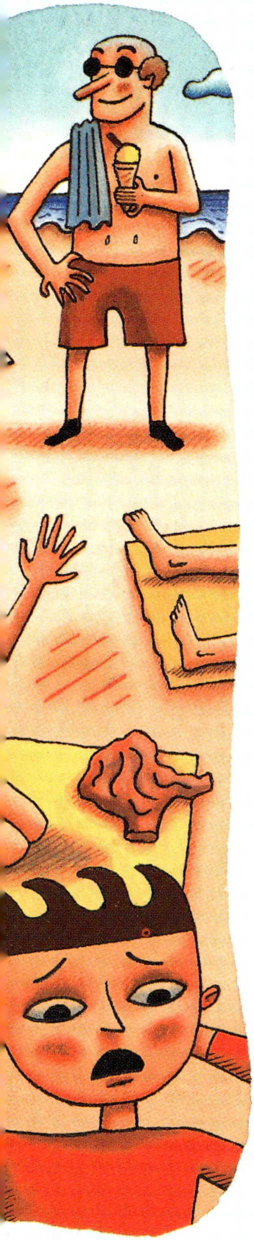

He Had to Go Home

Gregory panicked. What was he going to do? No way could he spend the night in the Griffons' house. They weren't his kind. He had to get away, to leave, right now. But what could he say to Felicia? He'd leave her a note, that's what. He could say something like "While you were swimming, I called home. I must return, right away. Sorry. I'll write soon." Before he'd always signed his notes and letters "Love, Greg." This time he'd just write "G." As if he was in a real hurry.

He always carried a small pad in his pocket. He took it out and scribbled the note, placed it on Felicia's towel and weighted it down with a small stone. Felicia was well out in the water, playing with some friends. She wouldn't notice him leaving. If she did, she'd think he was just going to get a soft drink or something.

He ran to the highway, hitched a ride with a truck driver—Greg couldn't stop himself from counting his twelve fingers—and got to the dock just in time to catch the next ferry across the bay. He bought his

ticket, handed it to the guard—who grasped it with his six fingers—and raced aboard.

Once he was safely underway, his stomach stopped churning. What a narrow escape, he thought. Thank goodness he and Felicia hadn't become any more involved with each other.

Again he stood on deck on the trip across the bay, straining to catch his first sight of Meckneb. Of course, he had to admit that he felt a little guilty, leaving just like that. He hoped he'd be able to explain it to Felicia someday. He'd have to write. For one thing, he had left his things behind. He'd have to ask Felicia to send them to him. From a safe distance, well, maybe they could still be friends, although right now he didn't think that was possible. He glanced back toward Brick City, now out of sight, and let out a sigh of relief. He wondered if his parents knew about the strange people of Brick City. If so why hadn't they warned him? And why hadn't Felicia told him that she was . . . that she was . . . he hated to use the word, but what else could he call it? She was *different*.

"What a strange condition," he mused. "But the really weird part is the two navels! I mean, how is it physically possible for anyone to have two navels? The extra thumbs—sure, that's strange enough. Still, it seems to me I have heard of people who were born with six fingers. Some English queen, I think. In fact, it may have been one of Henry VIII's wives. But two navels? That's really unheard of!"

When at last he saw the outline of his home city on the horizon, he glanced down at his own hands, resting on the boat's railing. He held them up and wiggled his fingers. He felt relieved, reassured. Almost as if he had feared he might have sprouted some extra ones. He would soon be home, back with his family, back in a town where everyone was normal—with four fingers on each hand and three navels, arranged in a pleasing triangle.

There's Nobody Else Like You

Each one of us is unique, and yet we all belong to the same species.

False Ideas of Difference

In the nineteenth century, human beings were classified into different races. Scientists of today say that the word "race" has little meaning. We are all basically the same.

Centuries of Research

For many centuries, people didn't know much about their bodies. They didn't understand how the brain worked, how food was digested, how the blood circulated, or even how children were conceived. Researchers are still making discoveries about the marvelous workings of the human body. When new diseases appear, researchers all over the world struggle to fight them.

People and Place

Where you live has a lot to do with who you are and the kind of life you will have. In many parts of the world there are children who do not get enough food. Perhaps the most dangerous continent on which to be born is Africa. Almost one African baby in ten dies in its first year of life. The average life span is only 53 years, compared to more than 70 years in Europe, Canada, and the United States.

Beliefs About the Body

The Kanakas of New Caledonia, an island in the south Pacific, believe that people and trees are made of the same material. Their word "karo" means both tree bark and human skin. The Dogons of Mali, in Africa, believe that the human body is "a piece of the universe."

An Envelope

Your skin is your body's largest organ. Far more than a covering, it has many roles.

Your Skin and You

When you look at your fingertips, you see small valleys, ridges, and swirls. Scientists believe that nobody else on Earth has fingerprints just like yours. Do you have dark skin? Light skin? It all depends on a substance called *melanin.*❦

❦***Melanin** is a brown-colored substance present in skin. It causes skin to darken when exposed to sunlight and protects skin from damage by ultraviolet light.*

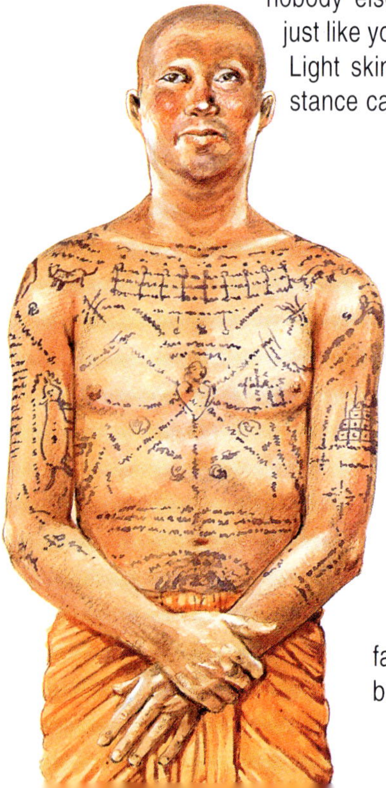

Tattoos

Designs that never disappear can be made by using needles to inject dye under the skin's surface. Most people get tattoos just for fun, but in more primitive societies, tattoos often have religious or magical meaning.

Your Skin Is Always Changing

Your skin is constantly being renewed. On the surface, cells die and wear away while new cells are being formed underneath.

# of Skin

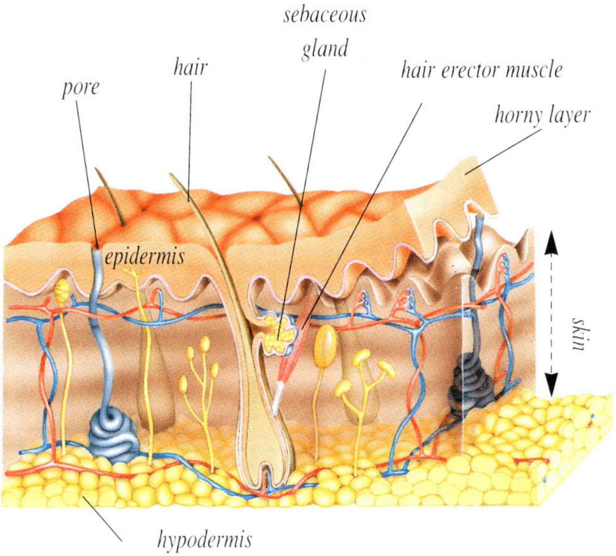

Your Skin Has Many Jobs

Your skin protects your body. It keeps out harmful bacteria. It prevents the loss of too much water. By sweating, skin maintains normal body temperature at about 98.6° F (37° C). Nerves in your skin give you your sense of touch.

You Skin Has Many Parts

The *cells* in the deepest layer of your epidermis (see illustration) multiply all the time. As they age, they move towards the surface, become harder, die, and flake off. The skin you can touch—the horny layer—is actually dead. There are glands in the skin that produce sweat to cool the body. Other glands, called *sebaceous,* produce oil that lubricates your skin. The hair erector muscles are what make hairs rise up and give you goosebumps.

Cells

Microscopic cells, grouped together in certain ways, make up all the parts of your body.

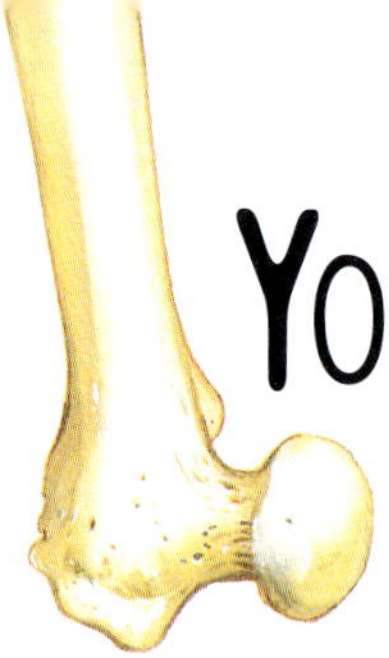

Your Framework of Bones

Your bony skeleton supports your body and protects your internal organs.

Basics About Bones

The bones in your body come in many shapes and sizes. Strong and tough, they are made mostly of minerals. To keep your bones healthy, you must eat foods containing enough minerals, especially calcium. The place where two bones meet is called a joint. Some joints can move, while some cannot. Those in your skull, for instance, are bound tightly together.

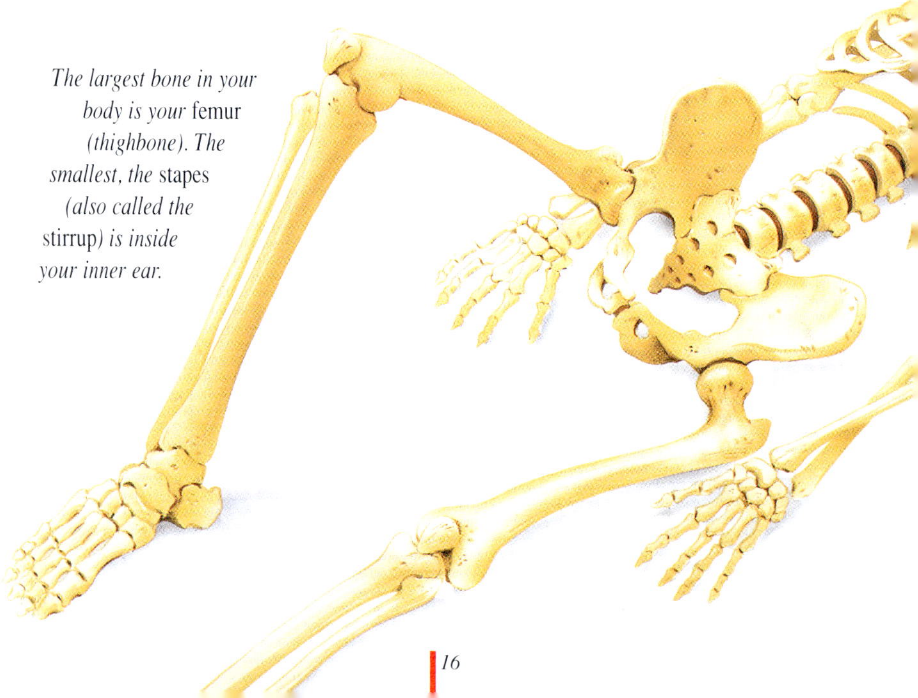

The largest bone in your body is your femur *(thighbone). The smallest, the* stapes *(also called the* stirrup*) is inside your inner ear.*

Bones Are Alive

Bones grow only in childhood but are alive throughout life. Bone cells are constantly renewed. If bones are broken, they can repair themselves. They make new bone cells to join the broken parts together.

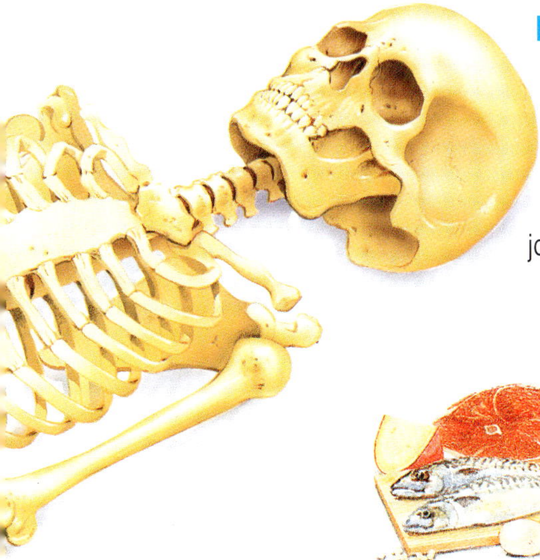

Diseases of the Skeleton

Poor diet can deform the bones of children. *Vitamin D* in your diet helps your bones grow properly. A disease called *arthritis,* caused by wear on the ends of bones in the joints, results in swelling and pain.

Vitamin D

This essential nutrient is found in dairy products, egg yolk, and fish. Your body manufactures vitamin D when your skin is exposed to sunlight.

Fossil

A fossil is the pattern, or the actual remains, of once-living material preserved in stone.

Fossil Bones of Long Ago

Many human bones have been preserved as *fossils* for thousands, even millions, of years. By studying fossil bones scientists have learned a lot about our ancestors.

How Do

Talking, walking, running, swimming—it is your muscles that make movement possible.

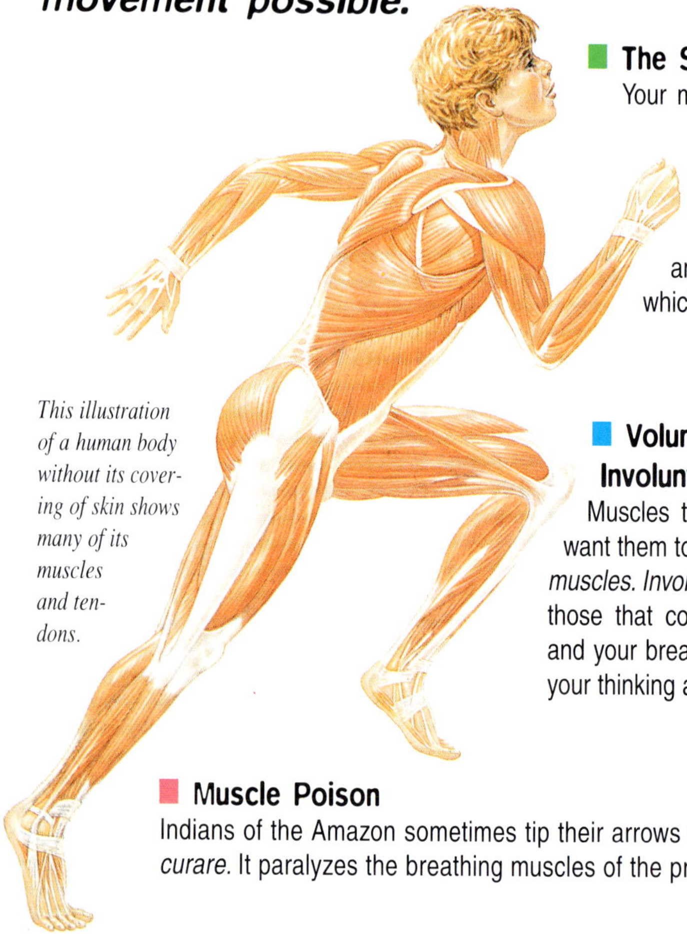

This illustration of a human body without its covering of skin shows many of its muscles and tendons.

The Skeletal Muscles

Your muscles are attached to bones by tendons. When you contract a muscle, it becomes shorter and moves the bone to which it is attached.

Voluntary and Involuntary Movement

Muscles that move when you want them to are called *voluntary muscles. Involuntary muscles*—like those that control your intestines and your breathing—move without your thinking about it.

Muscle Poison

Indians of the Amazon sometimes tip their arrows with a poison called *curare.* It paralyzes the breathing muscles of the prey they are hunting.

You Move?

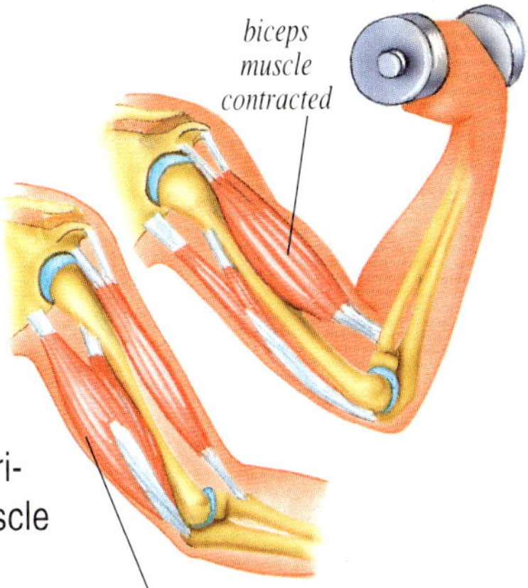

Pairs of Muscles

When you bend your arm, the biceps muscle contracts and the triceps muscle relaxes. When you straighten your arm the opposite happens. The triceps contracts and the biceps relaxes. Such muscle pairs control many body movements.

Ow! A Muscle Cramp

If you exercise or work too hard or long, your muscles might cramp. What has happened is that a chemical called *lactic acid* has been produced and too much lactic acid creates cramps. Massage or rest helps the muscle return to normal.

Shaping Your Body

Muscles that don't get enough exercise become smaller and weaker. Different activities develop different muscles. A right-handed tennis player will have a super strong right arm. A runner will have well-developed legs. When we speak of someone being in "good shape" we mean that all his or her muscles are strong.

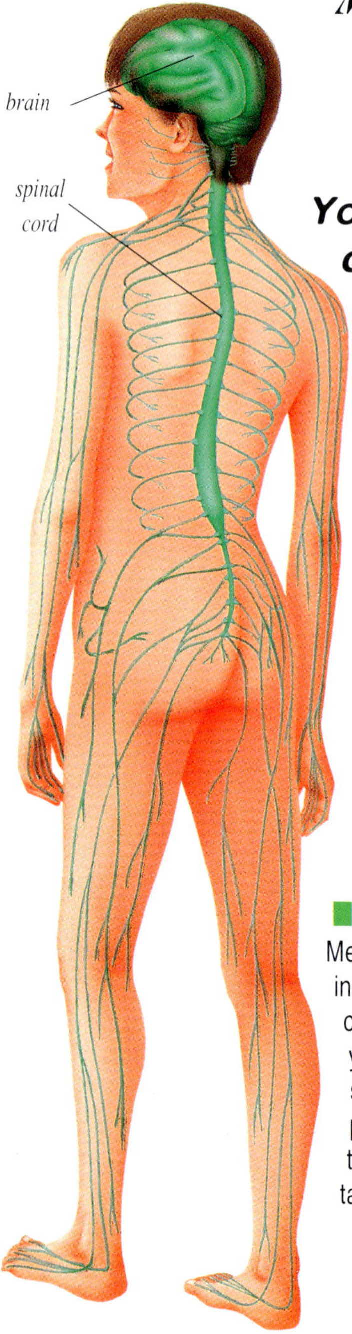

Your Nervous

You have a marvelous built-in communications and control system that is busy day and night.

Command Central: Your Brain

Have you ever solved a problem while you were sleeping? Some scientists say they have. Your brain never stops working, not even when you are asleep. It is constantly receiving messages from all your body's organs and sending back commands that control their activity. In the 3 pounds (1.4 kg) of tissue that forms your brain, there may be as many as 100 billion cells that enable it to perform this amazing work.

A Network of Nerves

Messages to and from the brain travel along an incredible network of nerves. The main "communications cable" of nerves runs from the base of your brain down your spinal cord. Along the way, smaller nerves branch out, going to different body parts. If all the nerves in your body were laid end to end they would make a line equal to the distance around Earth's equator.

System

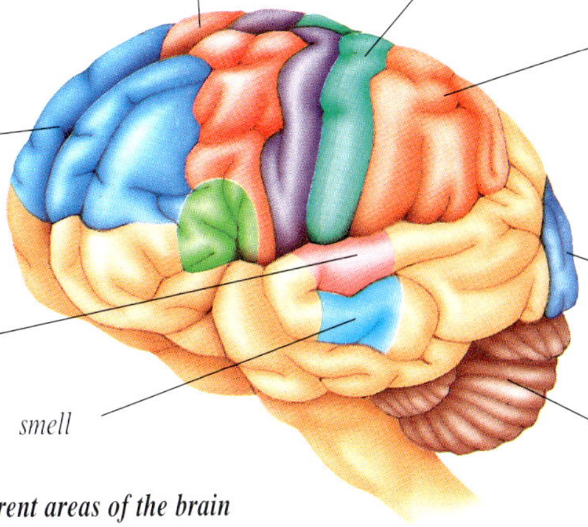

Different areas of the brain control different functions

Mapping Brain Function

They don't know it all, but scientists have learned a lot about the brain. The discovery that small brain *lesions* can cause problems led to the discovery that most human activities are controlled by very specific parts of the brain. The illustration above shows some of these locations.

Lesion
A small cut or other injury.

Speed Saves

Touch a hot iron and your hand automatically jerks away. This is called a reflex action. The message from your hand ("Hot!") travels to the nerves in your spine and up to the brain. An immediate message ("Pull away!") returns. It happens so fast that you may not get burned.

Test You

Make a Reflexometer

You will need:

- a piece of cardboard
- 7 markers in different colors
- a ruler

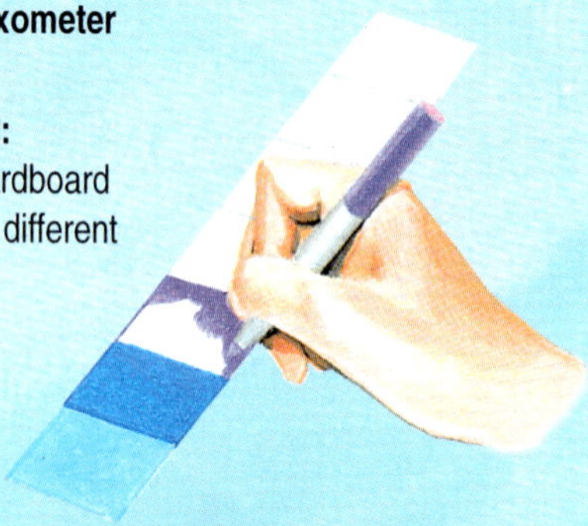

1. Cut a strip of cardboard about 2 inches by 12 inches (5 cm by 30 cm). Mark off 7 bands and color them.

2. Print the speed ratings on each band—the slowest at the top, the fastest at the bottom.

How to use the reflexometer.
Have a friend drop the cardboard strip. Try to catch it as fast as you can. The band your fingers close on gives you your rating.

Reflexes

Right or left?

1. Cross your wrists and place your palms together. Intertwine your fingers.

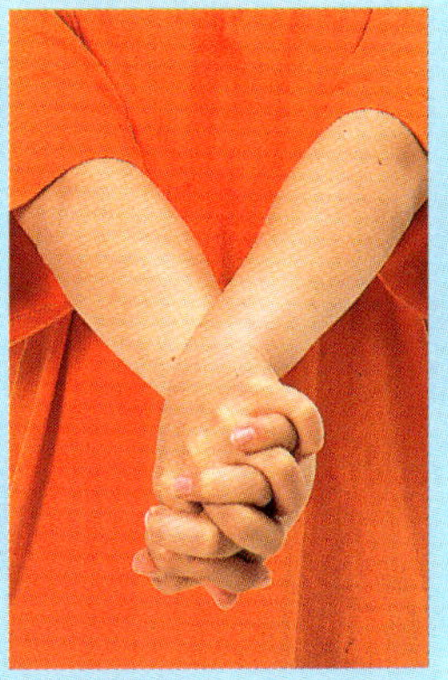

2. Raise your hands up in front of your chest.

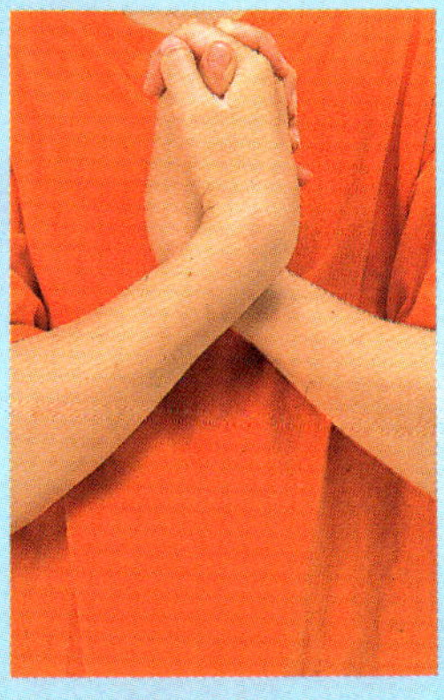

3. Ask a friend to point to one of your fingers without touching it. Try to move that finger. Hard, isn't it? Your brain sees the right on the left and the left on the right. You can't always believe what you see!

A Healthy Diet

Follow a few simple rules to eat the foods your body needs.

sugars

proteins

fats

Know What You Need

For growth and good health you must eat proteins, plentiful in meat, fish, and dairy products. For energy, you must have carbohydrates, found in grains and foods made from grain. Be careful not to eat too much fat, although even fats in moderate amounts are needed for good health.

Leafy green vegetables, carrots, tomatoes . . . these have lots of vitamin A.

Vitamins for Health

Vitamins are chemicals essential for life, even though you need them in only small amounts. You can get the vitamins you need by taking a daily pill, but the best way is to eat a well-balanced, varied diet every day.

More Fruits and Vegetables!

Doctors warn us that we do not eat enough fruits and vegetables. Many of our early ancestors may have eaten a diet much higher in these foods than most people eat today. Fruits and vegetables are rich in essential *minerals* and provide fiber, which is necessary for good digestion. A balanced diet is one that gives you the right kind of food in the right amounts.

Minerals
Substances—such as calcium, magnesium, phosphorus, potassium, and iron—that occur naturally in the earth.

A well-balanced meal

A poorly balanced meal

You Are What You Eat

People have believed for a long time that they become like the food they eat. African hunters eat lion meat to become strong. Some people refuse to eat rabbits because they think such food might make them timid. What do you think? Does sugar make you sweet?

What Happens to the

Over a period of 24 hours, or slightly more, food is broken down in your digestive system and passes into your bloodstream.

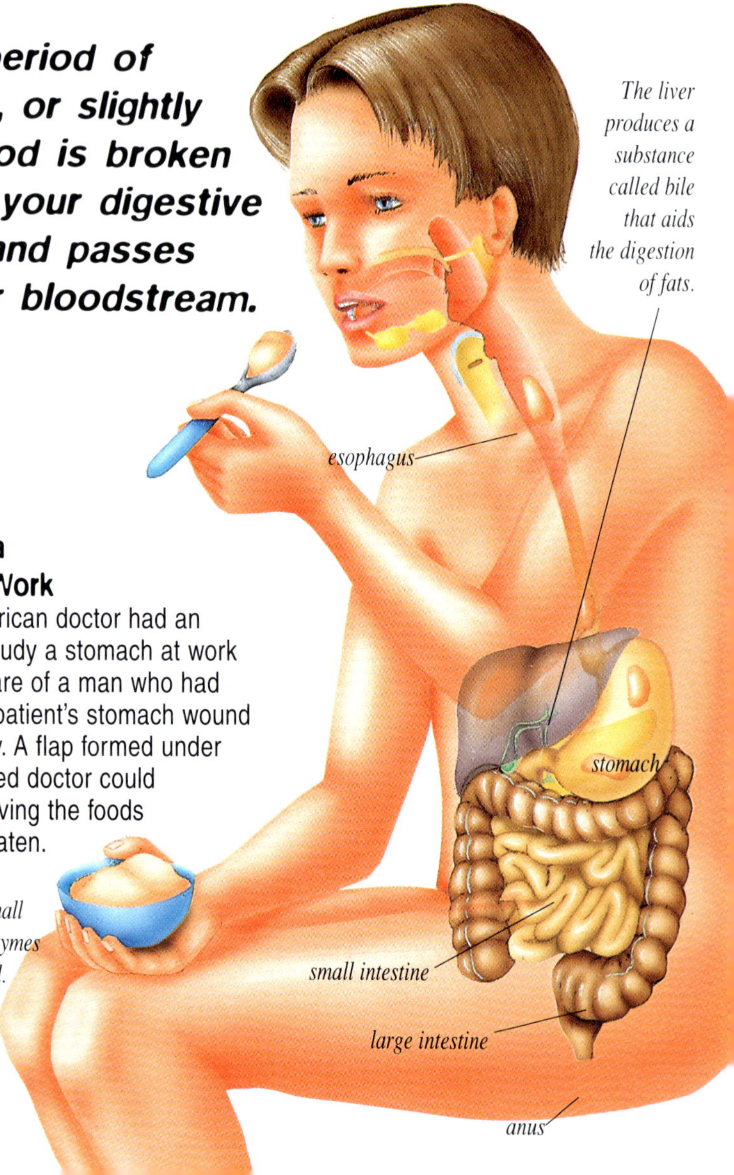

The liver produces a substance called bile that aids the digestion of fats.

Watching a Stomach at Work

In 1822 an American doctor had an opportunity to study a stomach at work when he took care of a man who had been shot. The patient's stomach wound healed strangely. A flap formed under which the amazed doctor could see acids dissolving the foods that had been eaten.

The pancreas and small intestine produce enzymes that break down food.

The digestive process works an average of 18 hours a day.

Food You Eat?

Tummy Rumblings

If your stomach is empty for too long, it fills up with gas. When the muscles of your stomach wall contract, your tummy rumbles. Time to eat!

Teeth

By about the age of 6, most children have 20 teeth—8 incisors, 4 canines, and 8 molars. When these "baby teeth" come out, they are replaced by permanent teeth. Most adults have either 28 or 32. The number varies because not everyone gets the four back molars.

Bottom teeth, adult

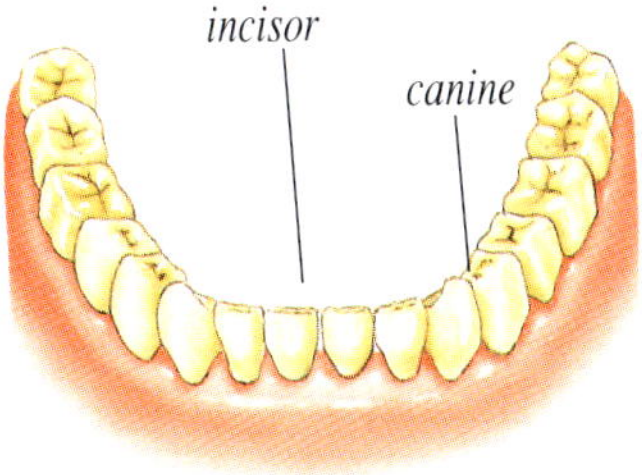

A 30-foot (9-meter) Journey

Digestion begins in your mouth, as soon as you start chewing. Saliva contains *enzymes*, which begin the process of digestion. The food you swallow then begins a 30-foot (9-meter) journey through the body. It ends when fecal matter is passed out through the anus. Along the way, food goes through a number of marvelous organs that change it to forms needed for nutrition. In the stomach, food is squeezed and mixed with acids. In the small intestine, other chemicals continue the food's breakdown. Most necessary food elements are absorbed into the bloodstream through the walls of the intestines.

Enzymes
Chemicals produced by the body that aid in the breakdown of food eaten.

Your Heart and

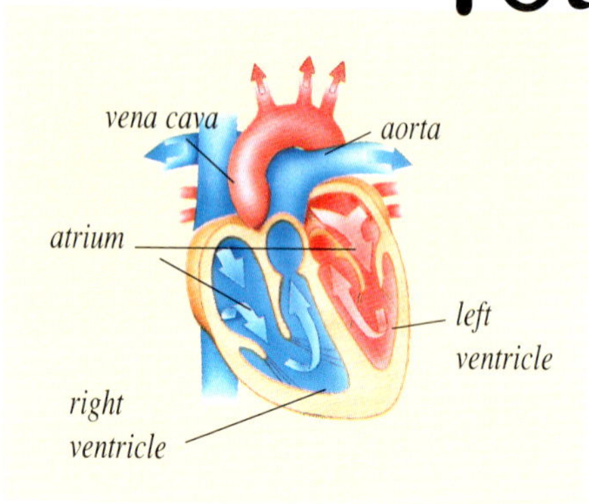

Your heart pumps life-giving blood to all parts of your body.

A Wonderful Muscle, Your Heart

The chemicals in the food you eat and the oxygen in the air you breathe wouldn't do you much good if there was no way to get them to the bodily organs that need them. That is the job of the heart. This marvelous muscle, which usually keeps pumping tirelessly more than once a second for decades, keeps nutrient-rich blood circulating to all parts of your body.

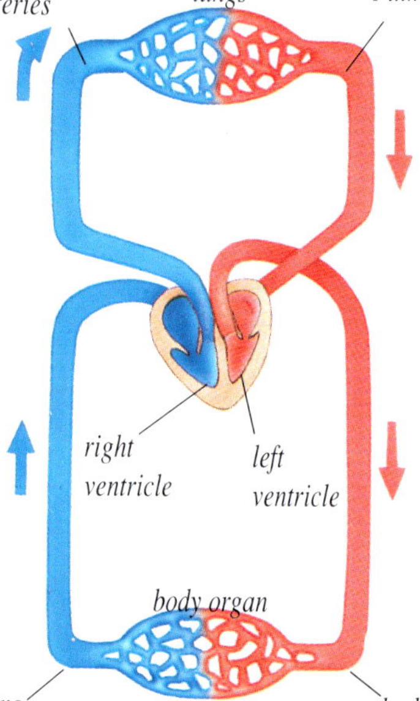

in blue: blood going to the heart or lungs.

in red: blood coming from the heart or lungs.

When you exercise hard your heart might beat as fast as 120 times a minute.

Circulatory System

How Your Blood Circulates

It is said that an average adult human has about 30 billion blood cells. Pushed by the pumping of the heart, they travel constantly throughout the body via a system of veins and arteries. Oxygen-depleted blood returns to the heart through the veins. It is next sent to the lungs where it gives up carbon dioxide and takes on oxygen. Then it is sent back to the heart, which pumps it out through the arteries.

Bloodletting

Doctors once believed that some patients would be helped if some of their blood was removed. The procedure was called bloodletting. Sometimes blood-sucking leeches were placed on the patient's skin. Sometimes veins were cut open and allowed to bleed.

Blood Transfusions

Doctors of today are more likely to save their patients' lives by giving them more blood—a process we call blood transfusion. The four main blood types are labelled A, B, AB, and O. Do you know what your blood type is? If you ever need a transfusion, doctors must be careful to match the blood they are giving you with your own blood. Don't worry—they'll check very carefully.

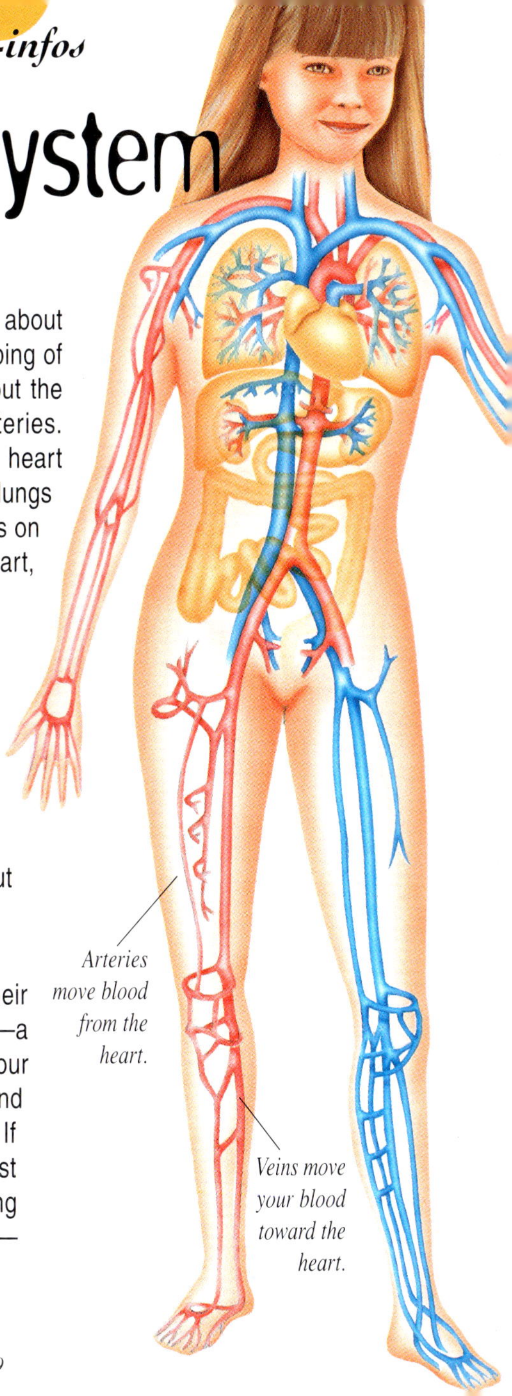
Arteries move blood from the heart.
Veins move your blood toward the heart.

A Very Busy Hospital

Somewhere in this hectic hospital scene there are two men who are twins. Can you find them? Clue: One wears his hair tied back in a ponytail, the other does not, but they have on identical ties.

Solution on page 63.

AZI
BEO

The

Breathing brings oxygen from air into the body, where it is burned to provide energy.

Two Remarkable Balloons, Your Lungs

Take a deep breath and feel air fill your lungs. Through the walls of your lungs, oxygen will pass into your blood. The oxygen will be exchanged for a waste product, carbon dioxide, which you then exhale.

When you inhale, a muscle group called the diaphragm works with the muscles of the ribcage to expand your chest cavity, pulling air into your lungs. When you exhale, the chest cavity contracts, pushing air out of your lungs.

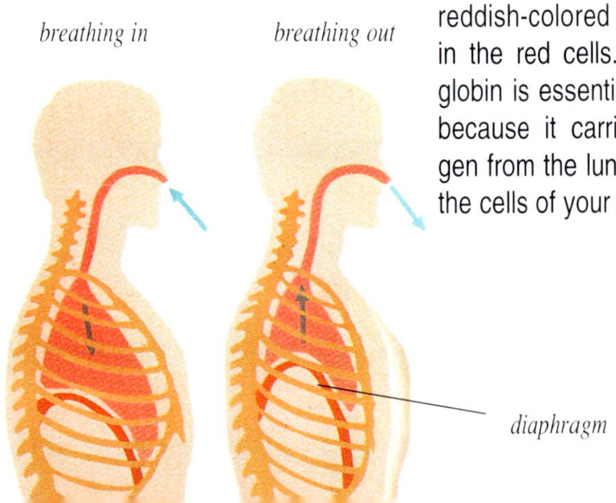

Why Is Blood Red?

Blood contains white blood cells and red blood cells. It gets its color from hemoglobin, the reddish-colored protein in the red cells. Hemoglobin is essential to life because it carries oxygen from the lungs to all the cells of your body.

Breath of Life

Air Pollution and Your Lungs

We must do everything we can to fight air pollution because it is menacing all life on Earth. Dust, smoke, and smog damage lungs, causing asthma and other diseases. Just inhaling other people's tobacco smoke can cause lung cancer.

Do All Animals Need Oxygen?

Yes, but they get it in different ways. Insects have a system of tubes that brings oxygen directly to the cells of their bodies. Fish take water into their mouths and pass it out their gills. This extracts the oxygen from the water before it leaves the fish's body.

Two Filters, the Kidneys

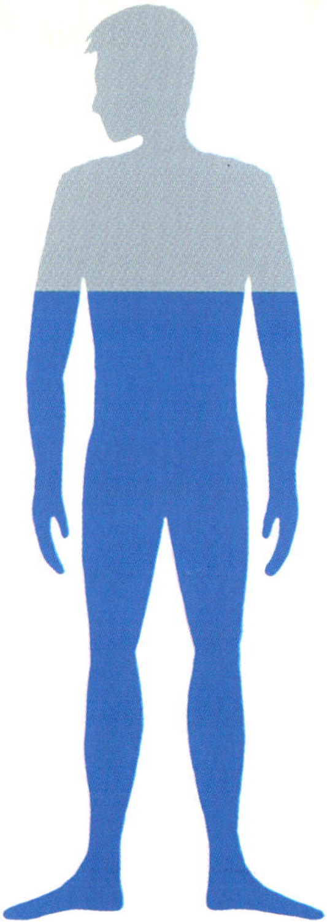

Your body weight is about 65 percent water.

Your two kidneys, each about the size of a young child's fist, clean poisons from your blood.

Kidneys Control Water Balance

By producing more or less urine, your kidneys control the amount of water in your body.

How Kidneys Purify Your Blood

During its journey around your body, your blood passes through the kidneys. They contain little tubes called *nephrons* that filter waste products from the blood. Mixed with water, these waste products form urine, which collects in a bag called the *bladder.* An adult passes about six cups of urine a day.

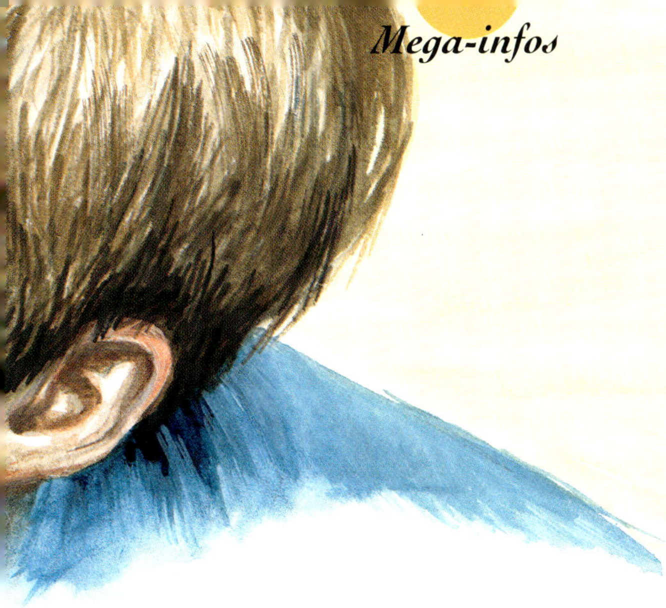

Medical Clues in Urine

Doctors have long known that a person's urine reveals a lot about the state of his or her health. They checked patients' urine for color, odor, and clarity. Hundreds of years ago, a king of France had his urine looked at every single day. Tests then were simple. Today, if you become ill and your doctor asks for a sample of urine, it will be sent to a laboratory for analysis.

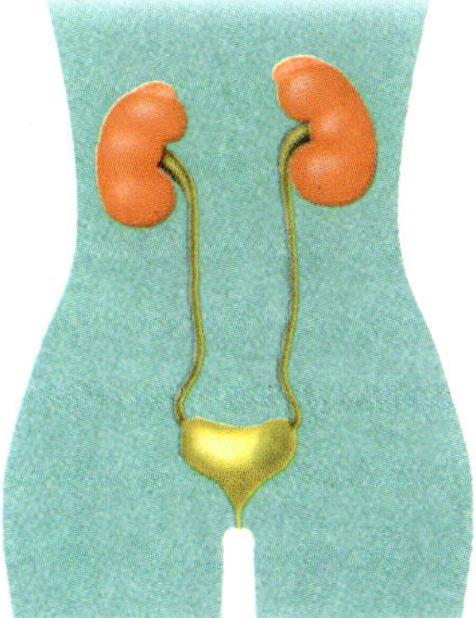

Artificial Kidneys

Even though you have two kidneys, one is enough to keep you alive and healthy. If both of your kidneys were to fail, you would either have to receive a kidney transplant or have special treatments at a clinic or hospital to remove the wastes from your blood.

A Well-

Body temperature and blood sugar levels are kept nearly constant.

Why Is There Sugar in Your Blood?

Blood sugar, in the form of *glucose,* provides body cells with energy. Some cells use only sugar for their fuel. This is the case with nerve cells, which need a constant supply of glucose.

Regulating Blood Sugar Levels

The liver and the pancreas are the most important regulators of blood sugar levels. The pancreas produces a chemical called *insulin,* which causes the liver to remove sugar from the blood. When blood sugar gets too low, the pancreas stops making insulin, and the liver releases sugar into the blood. Both high and low levels can be harmful. If blood sugar falls too low, essential cells can begin to die. If blood sugar remains too high, as in the case of uncontrolled diabetes, it can destroy the functioning of many bodily organs.

Regulated Machine

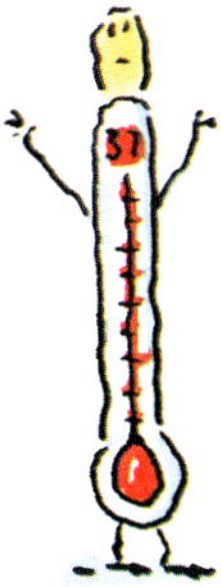

Cold or Hot?

Whether the air around you is cold or hot, your body temperature stays very near 98.6 degrees F (37 degrees C). A part of the brain called the *hypothalamus* is responsible for controlling body temperature. If the body needs cooling, sweat is produced. To warm our bodies we shiver or move around. Sometimes, of course, we become ill and body temperature rises. Fevers are a means of killing germs.

What About Animals?

Only mammals and birds keep a fairly constant body temperature. All other animals have body temperatures that vary according to the surrounding temperatures. Reptiles are active only when it is warm. Snakes become sluggish and inactive when the weather is cold.

Incredible

ASLEEP ON YOUR FEET

Did you ever fall suddenly asleep during the day, maybe even while you were standing up? Perhaps you hadn't slept enough the night before. But some people are victims of a rare condition called *narcolepsy.* No matter what they are doing, and even though they've had plenty of sleep, they may suddenly doze off. Though it is little understood, narcolepsy can be treated with medication.

MYSTERIOUS MUMMIES

Do you know how—and why—the Egyptians made mummies? Here's the why: Egyptians believed in an eternal life after death, which required an intact human body. Here's the gruesome how: Hooks were used to stir the brain into a sort of soup that was removed through the nostrils! Preserving chemicals were then injected into the skull cavity. Internal abdominal organs were removed, and the body was dried, salted, and wrapped in cloth. It was then ready for its eternal journey.

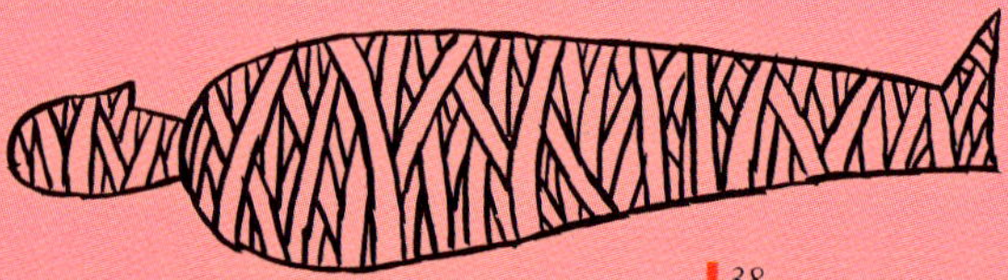

but True!

THE VILLAGE OF LONG LIFE

In the 1950s, scientists discovered a village—Vilcambra, Peru—where the Indian inhabitants commonly lived to be 100 years old. Some people in the village made it to 120, maybe even longer. How come? The scientists think there are probably many reasons—the clean mountain air, the vegetarian diet, and the unhurried lifestyle. An American of Danish descent lived to the age of 115 years. There are several people in the world who claim to have lived longer, but this record is the only one that can be proved.

A DEDICATED PRIEST

Important discoveries about digestion in humans and other animals were made by an Italian priest, Lazzaro Spallanzani, in the late eighteenth century. Father Spallanzani wondered what happened to food as it passed through the body, so he conducted some unusual experiments. For one, he took liquid from the stomachs of birds, mixed it with seeds, and put the mixture in little tubes. To keep the tubes warm, he held them in his armpits for days. To study his own digestion he swallowed food that was packed in tiny tubes in which he punched holes. He recovered the tubes from his feces and observed what had happened to it.

Infection Alert!

Always on the alert, your immune system protects you against dangerous bacteria and viruses.

The microscope made it possible for scientists to observe tiny organisms too small for the unaided eye to see.

Bacteria Are Everywhere

Bacteria, tiny one-celled creatures that cause many illnesses, are everywhere—on your skin, in the water you drink, in the air you breathe. Sweat and tears contain substances that can kill bacteria, which sometimes get inside the body, often through a puncture or cut. White blood cells, the soldiers of the immune system, usually succeed in fighting them off.

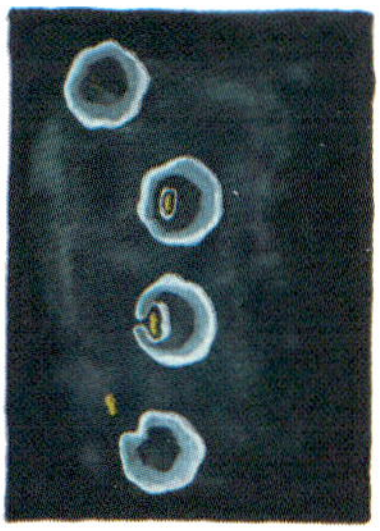

White blood cells destroy bacteria.

Dangerous Viruses

Scientists debate whether viruses are living organisms, but they all agree they are a threat to health. Colds and flu are caused by viruses. So are many more serious diseases, such as AIDS.

The Battle Against Disease

In 1796, an English doctor, Edward Jenner, observed that farm workers who caught a mild illness called cowpox never got *smallpox*, a far more serious disease. Jenner thought there might be a connection. He began to expose volunteers to cowpox by scratching their skin with pus from infected cows. Those scratched became mildly ill, but they did not catch smallpox. Jenner had discovered the process we call vaccination.

Smallpox
The last case of this deadly disease was in 1979.

Vaccination

Vaccination has saved many lives. By making people mildly ill, it stimulates their immune systems to ward off serious, even deadly, diseases. How many diseases have you been vaccinated against?

Sometimes children are born with very weak immune systems. They must be kept for a long time in sterile rooms, away even from their parents.

The Mystery of Sleep

You must sleep in order to be healthy. You will probably sleep more than a third of your life.

Light Sleep, Dream Sleep

When you first fall asleep, you enter a period of light sleep. You will lie quite still, your eyes will not move, and your breathing will be even. During this time, even slight sounds might wake you. But then comes a change. You enter what is called *REM (Rapid Eye Movement)* sleep. Your eyes move rapidly, your breathing becomes more irregular, and you are not easily awakened. Most dreams occur during REM sleep. Periods of light sleep and REM sleep alternate. The length of REM sleep periods usually increases as the night wears on.

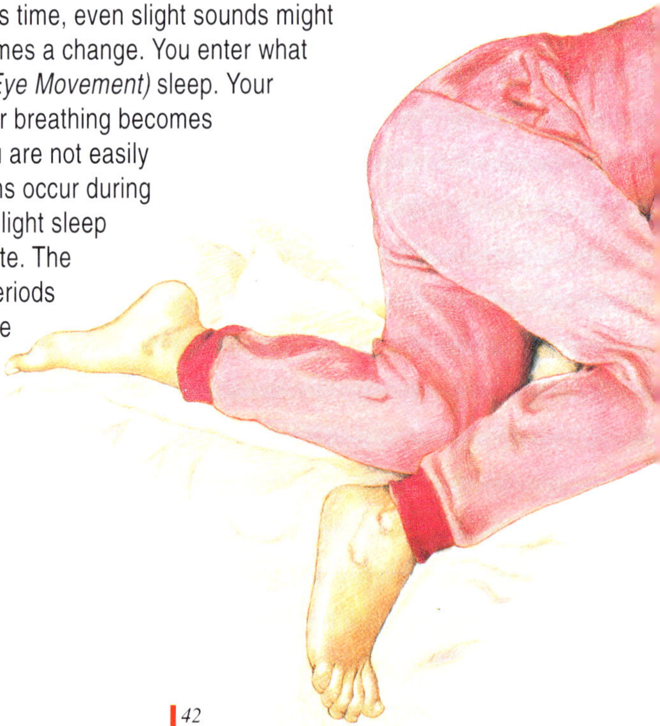

Why Must You Sleep?

Scientists still don't know exactly why, but they do know that a person deprived of sleep would die within a few weeks. Of course we know that sleep provides rest and helps you recover from fatigue. It may also be necessary to help your brain process and record things you have learned and experienced. Young people need more sleep than adults, so be sure to get your zzzzz's.

Light sleep and REM sleep are experienced by some animals. A horse sleeps 2 to 3 hours a night, a bat 19 to 20 hours a day.

Some animals sleep for months at a time! Such sleep during winter is called hibernation.

Sleep Walking

Do you ever walk in your sleep? Many people do. Some have even left their houses and walked city streets. After successfully avoiding obstacles, they returned to their beds. When they woke up in the morning they remembered nothing of their sleepwalking adventure.

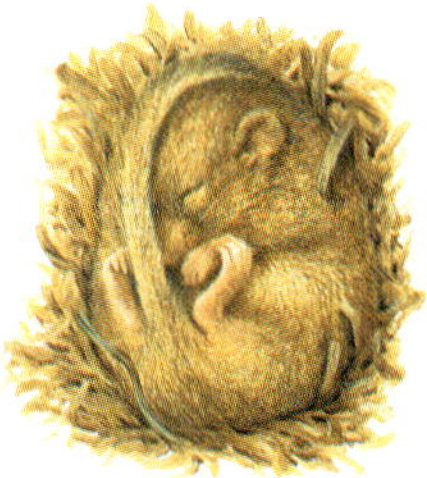

Your Five

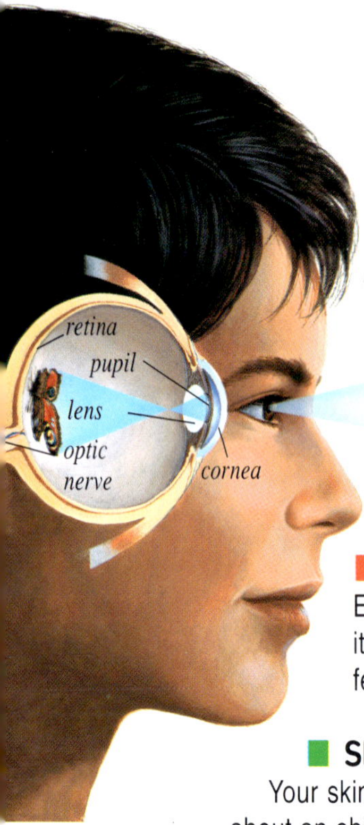

Your amazing senses send information about the outside world to your brain.

No Brain, No Sensations

Each of your sense organs sends your brain messages that it translates into smells, sounds, tastes, images, and the feel of things.

Skin to Feel With

Your skin contains sensitive nerves that tell the brain many things about an object touched—if it is hard, soft, sharp, cold, hot.

Eyes to See With

The *pupil* of your eye receives light reflected from an object you are looking at. The light reaches the *retina* behind the eye in the form of an upside-down image. The *optic nerve* sends this picture to the brain, which turns it right side up.

Two-eyed humans see white daisy petals against green grass. Bees, with 5 eyes, see the flowers as blue-green and the grass as pale yellow.

Senses

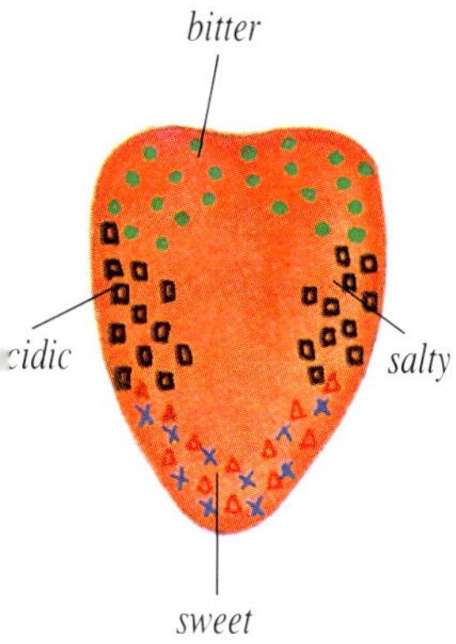

A Tongue to Taste With

Your tongue is covered with tiny bumps, the taste buds, which detect the flavors of foods. The buds can recognize only four kinds of flavor: bitter, sweet, salty, and acidic. It is the many combinations of these four that make the different tastes we sense.

A Nose to Smell With

Phew! Mmmmm! Your nose captures odors, good and bad. It is an aid to your sense of taste. Even pizza doesn't taste like much when you have a stuffed-up nose.

Ears to Hear With

When sound enters your ear and hits your eardrum, it affects many things, among them tiny bones called the *hammer,* the *anvil,* and the *stirrup;* liquid-filled canals; and nerves that send messages to the brain. It is your brain that interprets the sound and tells you what you are hearing—a strumming guitar, a cheering crowd, whispering.

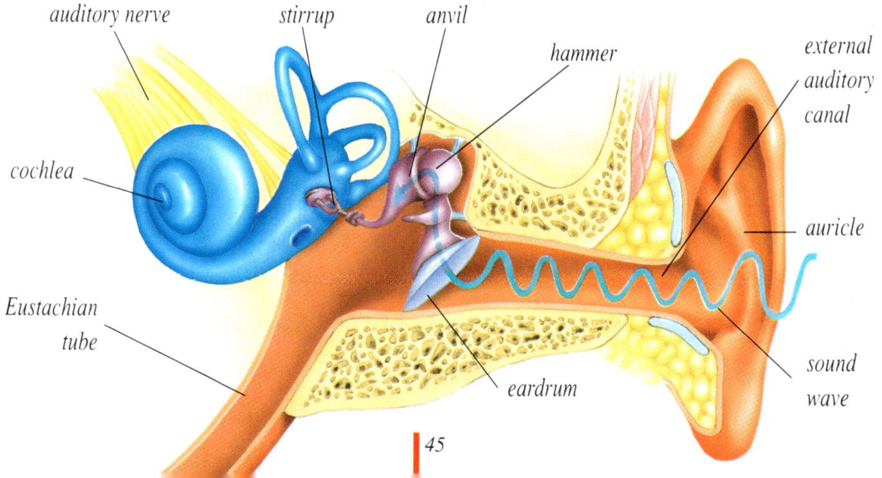

Fun with

Vision

You will need:
- a button
- a small bowl

Cover one eye and direct a friend to drop the button in the bowl by saying "left a little . . . now back a bit," etc. When the button drops, you will see that one eye is not as good as two.

Taste and Smell

You will need:
- some cheese, a carrot, an apple
- a knife
- a blindfold

1. Cut the foods into small pieces.

2. Blindfold a friend and have him hold his nose.

3. Offer him a bite of each food. Can your friend tell one food from another?

Your Senses

Hearing

Stand about a hundred feet (30 meters) away from a friend. Ask her to hit a hard object with a strong stick or piece of metal. You will notice that your eyes see the blow before your ears hear the sound.

Touch

1. Cut some small cards out of light-weight cardboard.

2. Print letters on the cards. With the point of a pencil, punch holes along the outlines of the letters.

3. Turn the cards over and give them to a blindfolded friend. Can she "read" the letters?

Male and

The differences in the bodies of men and women make it possible for them to create new life.

The Sexual Organs of a Male

Beginning at *puberty*, the testicles make *semen,* a liquid that contains millions of reproductive cells called *sperm*. Semen is ejected from the penis during sexual activity.

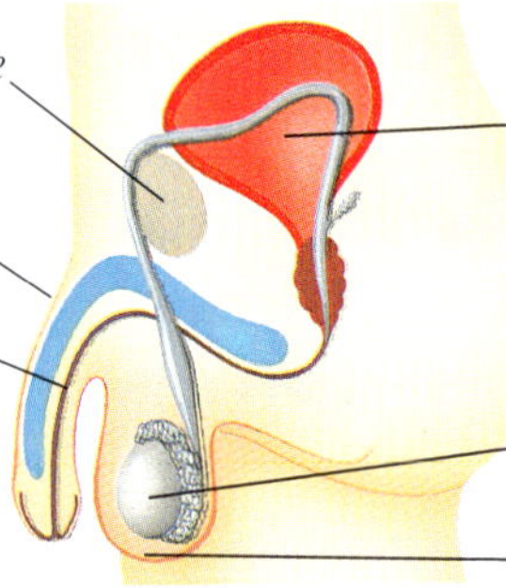

Puberty
The period in life during which a child's body gradually changes into that of an adult.

The Sexual Organs of a Female

A woman has two *ovaries*, a *uterus,* and a *vagina* which permits entrance by male sperm and exit for a baby being born. Each month, from puberty until *menopause*, an ovary releases an egg cell. It travels through a *Fallopian tube* to the uterus. If an egg cell has been fertilized, it remains in the uterus.

Menopause
That time of life, at about 50 years of age, when a women's ovaries stop releasing egg cells and her periods cease.

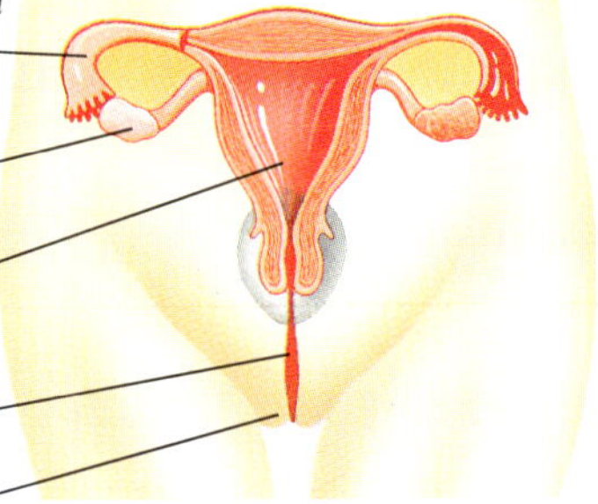

Female Bodies

Menstrual Periods

Each month, if no new life is conceived, the blood swelling the uterus in preparation for a fertilized egg is no longer needed and drains out the vagina. The time that this takes is called a woman's *period.*

Conceiving New Life

When a man and a woman love each other, they have a strong desire to be physically close and to have sexual intercourse. When they do, sperm is ejected into the woman's vagina. If a sperm cell reaches an egg cell, they unite and conception occurs. What forms then is the first cell of a future baby.

Amazing Hormones

The sexual functioning of both men and women is controlled by chemicals called *hormones.* Males have greater amounts of the male hormone, *testosterone.* Females have more of the female hormone, *estrogen.*

Nine Months to

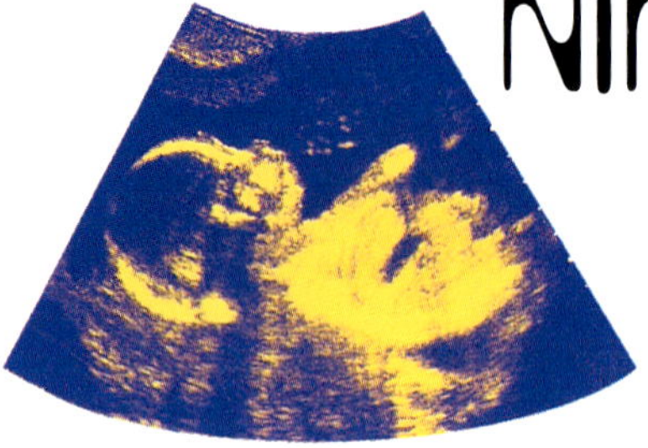

An ultrasound❦ picture of an unborn baby.

Well protected in its mother's uterus, a baby develops little by little.

Pregnancy

A pregnant woman should take good care of her health. Her unborn child gets its nourishment through the *umbilical cord* that connects mother and baby. Doctors are able to see a developing baby by using a machine that makes pictures with sound waves. By its twenty second day, the heart is beating. By the third month, legs and arms have formed. As it nears the end of the nine months, a baby is usually head down—the best position for birth.

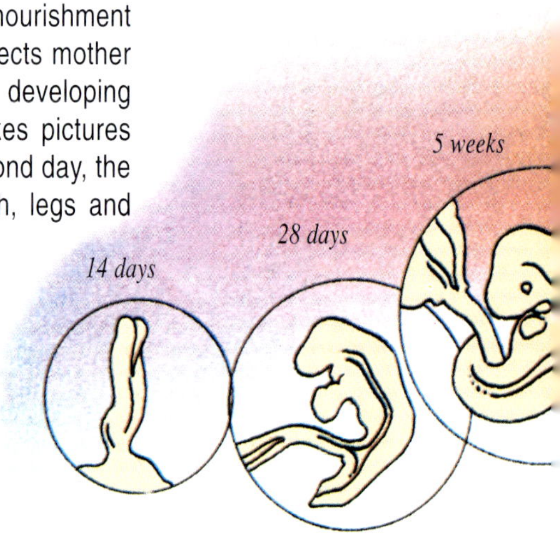

❦Ultrasound scanner
A machine that uses sound waves to make a picture of a developing baby.

Misconceptions

It was not until the eighteenth century that it was understood that a female egg cell and a male sperm cell had to unite to create a baby. Sperm was not even discovered until 1677. In the seventeenth century some biologists thought that the sperm contained a baby in miniature.

Make a Baby

Safe in the Uterus

The fertilized egg is moved along to the uterus, a journey that takes about seven days. There it stops and gradually becomes surrounded by a fluid in which it will grow for nine months.

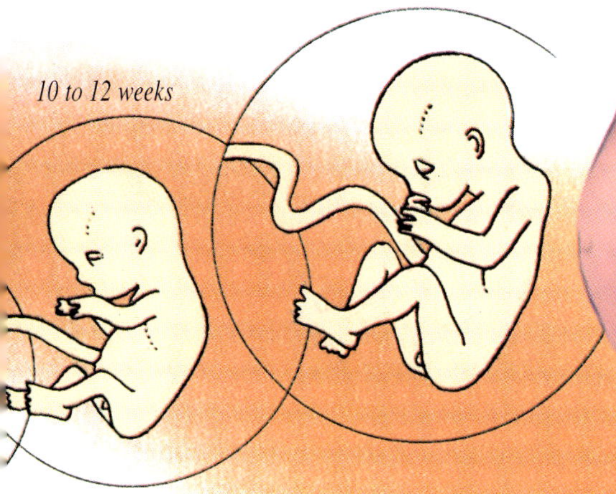

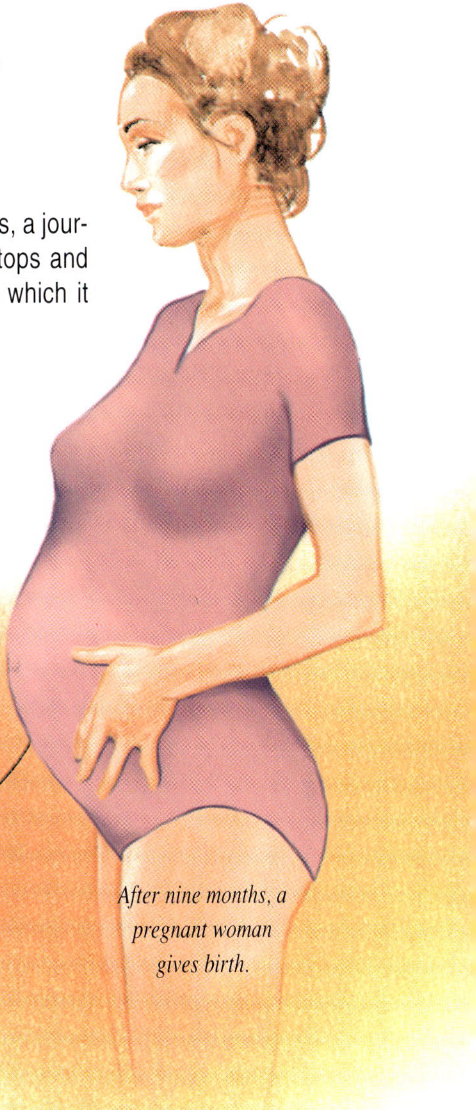

After nine months, a pregnant woman gives birth.

When two babies are formed from a single egg, they are identical twins. Non-identical twins develop from two eggs fertilized at the same time.

The First Minutes of Life

After nine months of waiting, the great moment arrives. A new human being is about to enter the world.

The Birth Process Begins

When a woman feels repeated contractions of her uterus, she knows it is time for her baby to be born. She may go to a hospital, or she may choose to have her baby at home with the help of a midwife.

The Birth

It may be many hours after the first contractions that a mother hears her baby's first cry. The mother's contractions continue until a spongy mass called the *placenta,* to which the umbilical cord is connected, is squeezed from the uterus and discharged through the vagina.

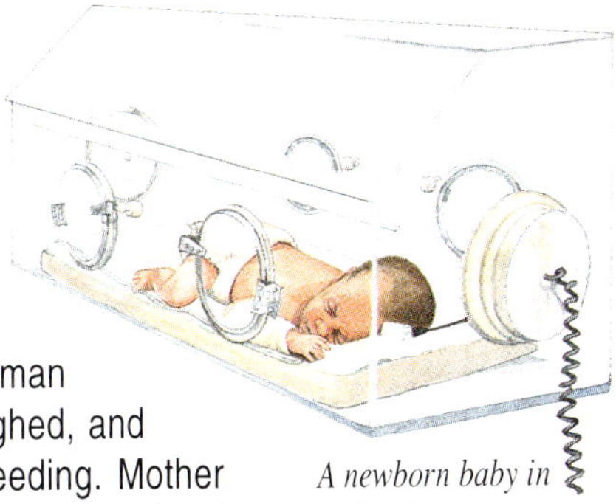

A newborn baby in an incubator.

What Happens Next?

Once the baby has taken its first breath and the umbilical cord has been cut, a new human life is on its own. The baby is washed, weighed, and placed at its mother's breast for the first feeding. Mother and child are no longer joined physically but a new bond begins—that of love.

When There Are Complications

If a woman's contractions go on for too long without the baby being born, a doctor may have to perform what is called a Caesarian—cutting through the abdominal wall to remove the baby. Sometimes a baby is born prematurely, before it is fully developed. The tiny infant has to be placed in an incubator for days or weeks.

Looking after

Good health depends on looking after yourself and not doing things that harm your body.

Keeping Fit

One way to stay healthy is to exercise regularly. Exercise keeps your muscles firm and helps your organs, particularly your heart and lungs, to work better. Playing sports, cycling, swimming, dancing—even walking to school—are all good forms of exercise. So start today—getting fit and staying fit will be fun.

Fighting Germs

There are always germs living on your skin and generally they do no harm. But if germs get into your body, they can make you ill. Germs can get onto food from dirty hands, so it is important to wash your hands before meals and after going to the bathroom. Germs also grow on bits of food left in between your teeth. Brushing your teeth after meals and before you go to bed at night helps to get rid of them.

Yourself

Avoiding Harmful Substances

Doctors prescribe drugs as medicine to make sick people better. But some young people use other kinds of drugs that are seriously dangerous to their health. They take the drugs to feel better about themselves, or be less shy, or feel they belong a group. In time, they may become so addicted to the drugs that they cannot live without them.

People who smoke cigarettes become breathless and may have a cough. That's because they are taking tar, nicotine, and poisonous gases into their body. These can also cause heart disease and lung cancer.

People who drink too much alcohol don't just get noisy and stagger around—they may eventually damage their liver.

You can enjoy life so much more if you stay well—so it really is better to avoid all of these harmful substances.

Not too much Sun

It's fun to be on the beach or in the park on a hot summer's day. Don't forget sunlight contains ultraviolet light that can burn the skin and may cause skin cancer. So when you are out in the sun, protect your skin with sunblock or cover up with some more clothing.

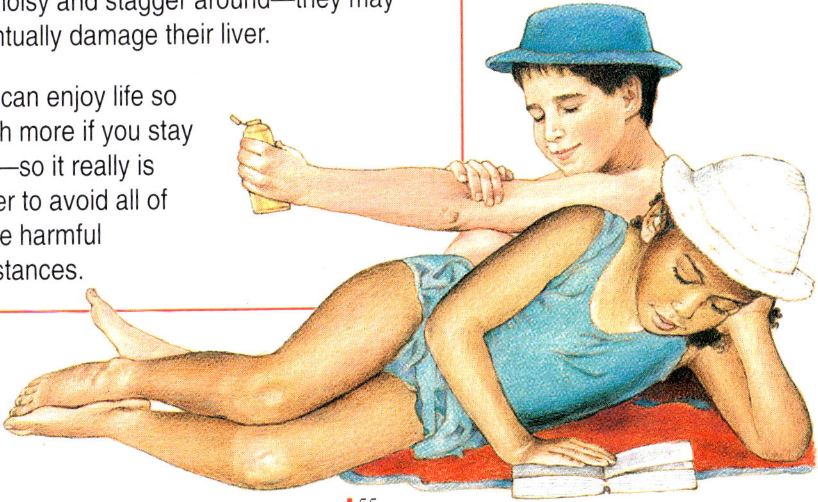

The Changes

During the period called* puberty, *as a child becomes an adult, life can seem difficult.

Profound Changes

At some time between the ages of 10 and 13, the body begins the series of changes that come with puberty. Not everyone begins puberty at the same age, but it usually begins in boys at about 12 years and in girls at about 11 years. It is very important to remember that these are just average figures. Don't be concerned if puberty begins somewhat earlier or later for you.

In adolescence, boys usually begin to be attracted to girls and girls to boys.

# of Adolescence

Boys During Puberty

As boys undergo puberty many changes occur. The sexual organs become larger, hair appears in the pubic area, under the arms, on the jaw, cheeks and upper lip. A boy's voice becomes deeper, his muscles grow larger. The first *ejaculations* (emissions of sperm) occur.

Girls During Puberty

As girls enter puberty their breasts grow larger, hair appears in the pubic area and under the arms, hips widen, and the first menstrual periods begin. At first, a girl's periods may not be regular but they become more so with time.

Other Changes

Some changes may be unpleasant, such as the eruption of pimples. Others may be emotionally difficult, such as moody behavior and embarassment about new sexual feelings. But these changes are normal and usually temporary. The adolescent is merely adapting to the beginning of a new, strange, wonderful adult life.

True or

The contractions of the heart are voluntary, not automatic.

False. You don't have to think about your heart beating. It does it strictly on its own.

The liver has nothing to do with digestion.

False. It produces bile, a substance essential for the digestion of fats.

Red blood cells are made in the marrow of certain bones.

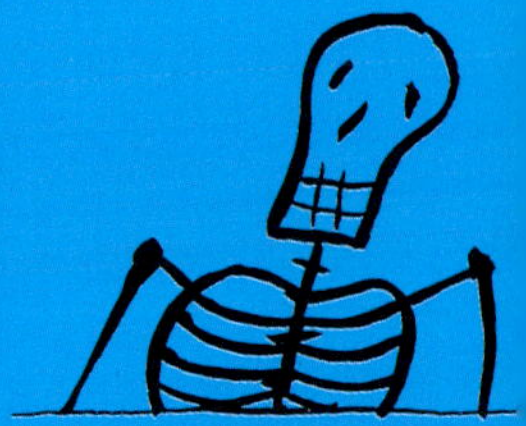

True. Red blood cells are made in the bone marrow of the skull, vertebrae, ribs, sternum, and iliac bones.

A child has more bones than an adult.

True—in a way. Certain small bones, which are separate in children, fuse together for form larger bones in adulthood.

False?

■ **Color-blind people confuse red and yellow.**

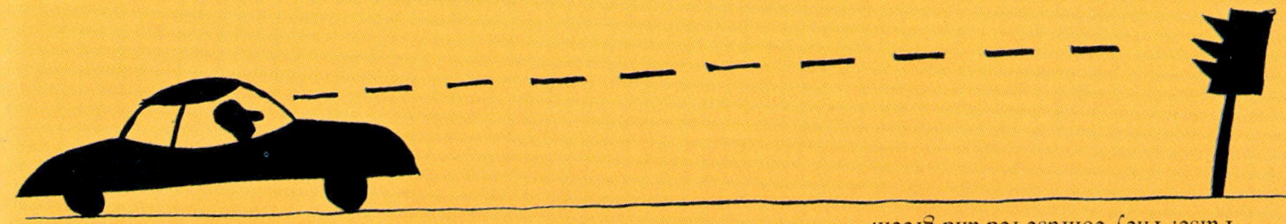

False. They confuse red and green.

■ **Near-sighted people have trouble seeing distant objects. Far-sighted people have trouble seeing nearby**

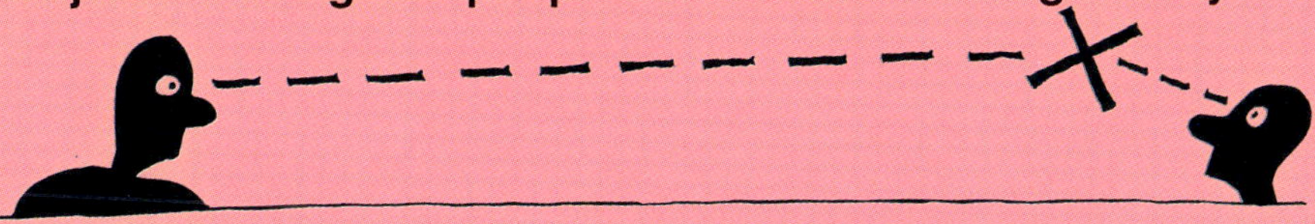

True. In both cases, vision can be improved by corrective lenses.

■ **Birth control pills protect against AIDS.**

False. Birth control pills can only prevent conception.

■ **Antibiotics are medicines that kill viruses.**

False. There are very few medications that can fight viruses. Antibiotics are effective only against bacteria.

Quiz

True or

■ **Blood sugar level can vary considerably without risk to health.**

False. It must be kept at about one gram of sugar per quart (liter) of blood.

■ **Oxygen is carried by white blood cells to all the cells of our bodies.**

False. It is the red blood cells that transport oxygen.

■ **When you sneeze, the air leaves your nose at about 100 miles (160 kilometers) per hour.**

True. Sneezing must be forceful to get rid of the dust and pollens tickling your nostrils.

■ **Tetanus is a disease for which there is no vaccine.**

False. Tetanus is a dangerous disease that can enter the body through a cut or puncture wound. You can and should be vaccinated against it.

False?

Water is indispensable to your body.

True. Water makes up about 65 percent of your weight. If you weigh 80 pounds (37 kg), your body contains approximately 52 pounds (23 kg) of water.

There is a lot of protein in pasta, rice, and bread.

False. Those are foods containing carbohydrates. The best protein-rich foods are meat, fish, milk, and cheese.

The navel is the scar left by the umbilical cord, which links an unborn baby to its mother.

True. And it is a scar that remains throughout life.

The body of an adult contains 50 million cells.

False. There are billions of cells in the human body!

Index

Adolescence, changes occurring in, 56
Africa, 13
AIDS, 41, 59
Air pollution, 33
Alcohol, dangers of, 55
Amazon, Indians of, 18
Antibiotics, 59
Anus, 27
Aorta, 28
Arteries, 28, 29
Arthritis, 17
Asthma, 33
Atrium, 28

Baby, beliefs about development of, 50
Bacteria, 40, 59
Birth, 52, 53
Birth control pills, 59
Bladder, 34, 48
Blood, 32, 40, 58, 60
  circulation, 29
Bloodletting, 29
Blood sugar, 36, 60
Blood transfusion, 29
Body temperature, 15, 37
Bones, 16, 17, 18, 58
Brain, 20, 21, 37, 38, 44, 45
Breathing, 32, 42

Caesarian, 53
Carbohydrates, 24, 61
Cells, 15
  blood, 32, 40, 58, 60
  egg, 48, 49, 50
  sperm, 48, 49, 50, 57
Colds, 41
Color blindness, 59
Conception, 49
Curare, 18

Diabetes, 36
Diaphragm, 32
Digestion, 26, 27, 39
Dreams, 42
Drugs, dangers of, 55

Ear, parts of, 45
Enzymes, 26, 27
Exercise, 54
Eyes, parts of, 44

Fetus, development of, 50
Fever, 37
Fingerprint, 14
Fish, oxygen intake, 33
Flu, 41
Food, 24, 25, 27
Fossil bones, 17

Germs, 54
Glands
  sebaceous, 15
  sweat, 15

Hearing, sense of, 45, 46
Heart, 28, 29, 58
Heart beat, frequency of, 29
Hemoglobin, 32
Hibernation, 43
Hormones, 49
Hospital, 30
Hypothalamus, 37

Immune system, 40, 41
Incubator, 53
Infection, 40
Insects, oxygen intake, 33
Insulin, 36
Intestines, 18, 26

Jenner, Edward, 41
Joints, 16

Kidneys, 34, 35

Lactic acid, 19
Life spans, 13, 39
Liver, 26, 58
Lungs, 29, 32, 33

Melanin, 14
Menopause, 48
Menstruation, 48
Microscope, 40
Mummies, 38
Muscles, 18, 19, 28, 55, 57

Narcolepsy, 38
Navel, 61
Nervous system, 20
Nose, 45, 60

Osteoarthritis, 17
Ovaries, 48
Oxygen, 32, 33, 60

Pancreas, 26, 36
Penis, 48
Placenta, 53
Pregnancy, 49, 50, 51
Prostate gland, 48
Puberty, 48, 56, 57

Race, 12
Reflex action, 21
Reflexes, test of, 22

Saliva, 27
Scrotum, 48
Semen, 48
Senses, 44, 45, 46, 47
Sexual intercourse, 49
Sexual organs, 48
Sight, 44, 46, 59
Skeleton, 16, 17
Skin, 14, 15, 40, 44
Sleep, 42, 43
  walking, 43

Smallpox, 41
Smell, sense of, 45, 46
Sneezing, 60
Spinal cord, 20
Stomach, 26, 27

Taste, sense of, 45, 46
Tattoos, 14
Teeth, 27
Tendons, 18
Testicles, 48
Tetanus, 60
Tobacco, 33, 55
Tongue, 45
Touch, sense of, 44

Ultrasound scanner, 50
Ultraviolet light, 14
Umbilical cord, 50, 53, 61
Urine, 34, 35
Uterus, 48, 49, 51, 52, 53

Vaccination, 41
Vagina, 48, 49, 53
Veins, 28
Vena cava, 28
Ventricles, 28, 29
Viruses, 40, 41
Vitamins, 17, 24

Water, percent in body, 34, 61

Answers to the puzzle on pages 30–31.

Photo credits for stickers

Kairos, Latin stock/Science Photo Library; J. Bavosi/Science Photo Library; L. Bobbe/Tony Stone Images; M. Kulyk/Science Photo Library; professors P. M. Motta, and S. Makabe/Science Photo Library; Petit Format; J. Stevenson/Science Photo Library.

Photo credits for picture cards

Top: M. Kulyk/Science Photo Library; E. Grave/Science Photo Library; C. Bjornberg/Science Photo Library; Colour Transparency/James davis travel Photography; Mary Evans Picture Library; M. Williams/Tony Stone Images; Bottom: J. Fortunato/Tony Stone Images; professors P. M. Motta, K. R. Porter and P. M. Andrews/Science Photo Library; Bridgeman Art Library; A. Hart-Davis/Science Photo Library; Rosenfeld Images/Science Photo Library.

Illustrations

Ian Chamberlain, Peter Dennis, Éric Doxat, Jeff Fisher, Pamela Goodchild, Daniel Guerrier, Sophie Jacopin, Chirstian Jégou, Urs Landis, Olivier Lemoine, Nathalie Locoste, Denise and Claude Millet, Michael Sheehy, Étienne Souppart, Joanna Williams

The title of the French edition is *Le corps humain exploré*
Published by Les Editions Nathan, Paris

Barron's edition adapted by Carlisle Associates.

All inquiries should be addressed to:
Barron's Educational Series, Inc.
250 Wireless Boulevard
Hauppauge, NY 11788

Library of Congress Catalog Card No. 97-77434
International Standard Book No. 0-7641-5093-6

Printed in Italy
9 8 7 6 5 4 3 2 1

Stickers

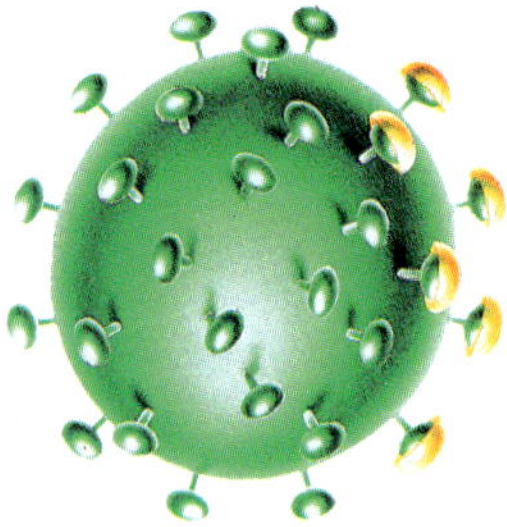

Model of the HIV virus

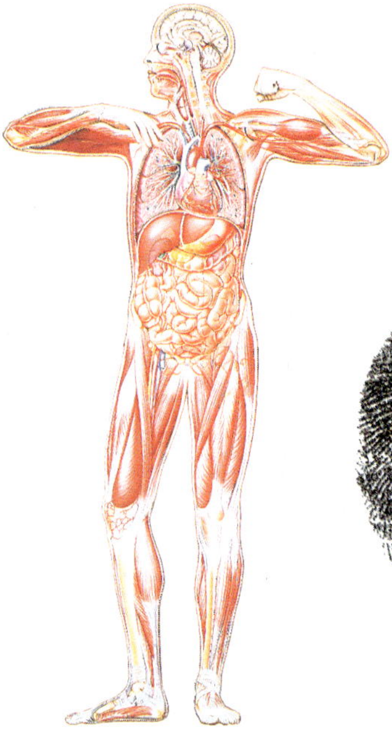

fingerprint

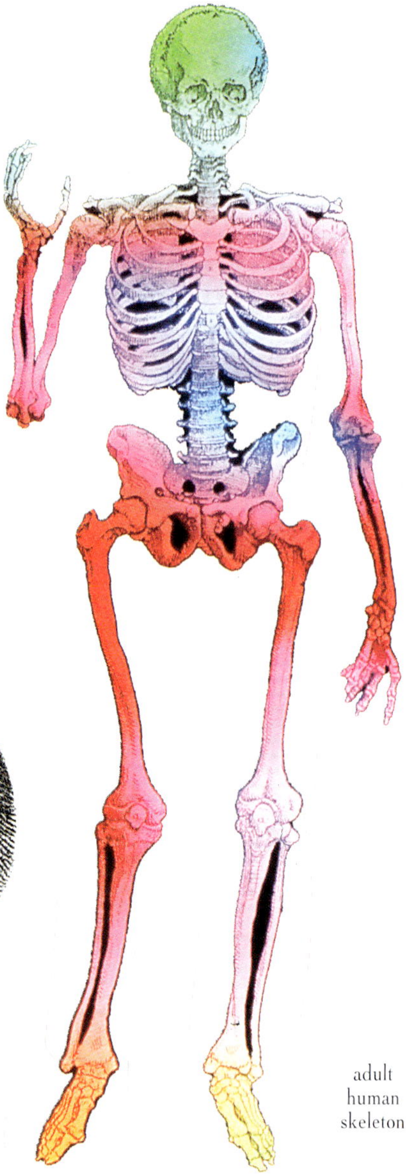

adult human skeleton

muscles and internal organs

Stickers

fetus at 6 weeks

infant at
3 to 4
months

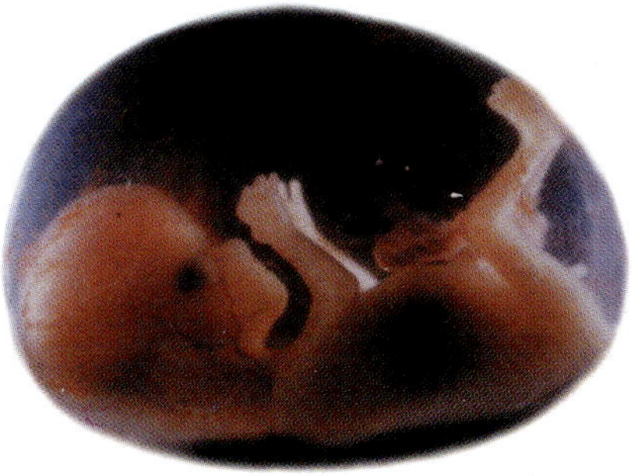

fetus at 4 months

infant at 6 to 8 months

short bone: vertebrae

long bone:
humerus

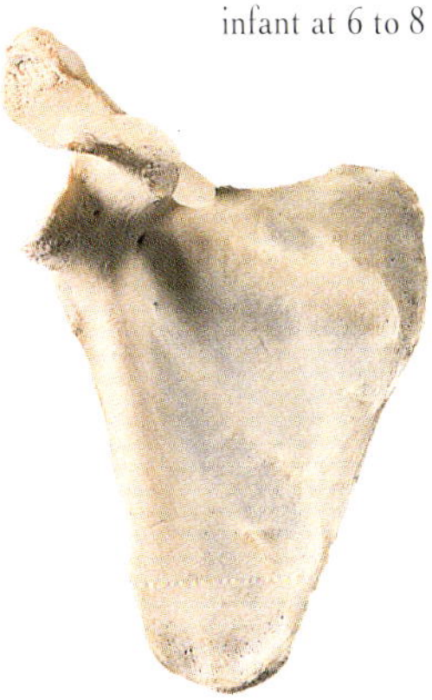

flat bone: scapula

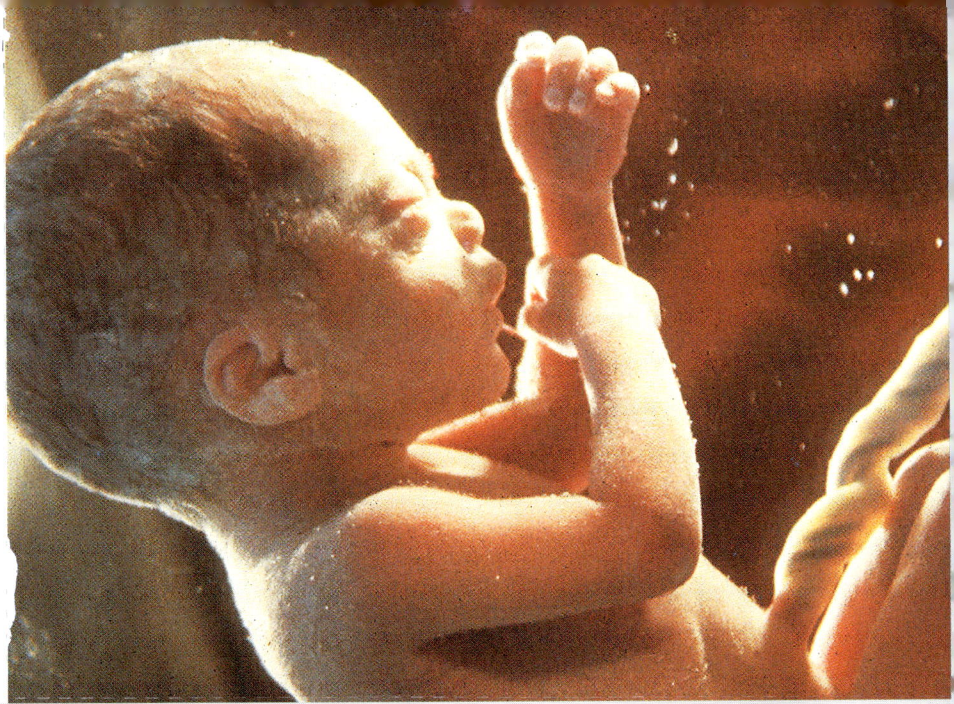

Picture Cards

A Fetus at 6 Months

At 6 months, the future baby is about 12 inches (31 cm) long and weighs almost 2 pounds (.9 kilogram). It sleeps 16 to 20 hours a day, moving from time to time and experiencing frequent hiccups.

Picture Cards

Children of the World

While people may look different and have skin that is dark, light, or in between, all human beings are basically the same. Scientists say that the distinction we call "race" really has little significance.

Picture Cards

Broken Finger

This X-ray of a hand shows a broken bone in one of the fingers. Broken bones are usually held in place by a cast until the break heals.

Picture Cards

Red and White Blood Cells

Red blood cells transport oxygen throughout the body. White blood cells, seen near the center of the photo, are the sentinels that destroy invading microbes.

Picture Cards

Tooth Puller

In days of old, teeth were pulled with pliers. This barbaric practice was carried out without the use of anesthetic. What pain!

Picture Cards

Hair

The principal ingredient of hair is a substance called *keratin.* Blood vessels bring nutrients to the roots of hair, stimulating its growth.

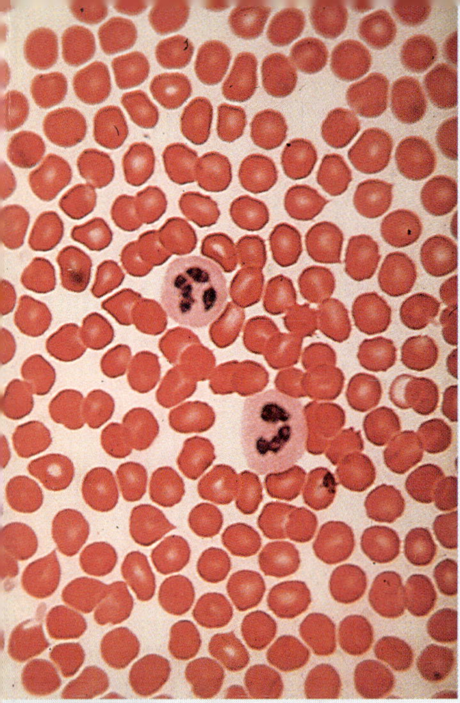
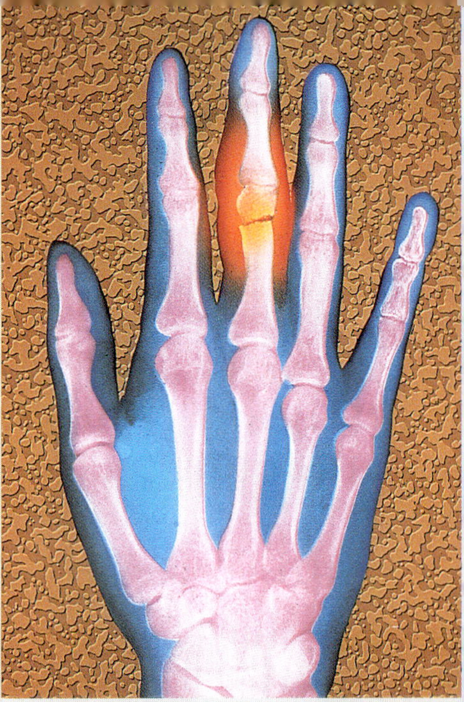
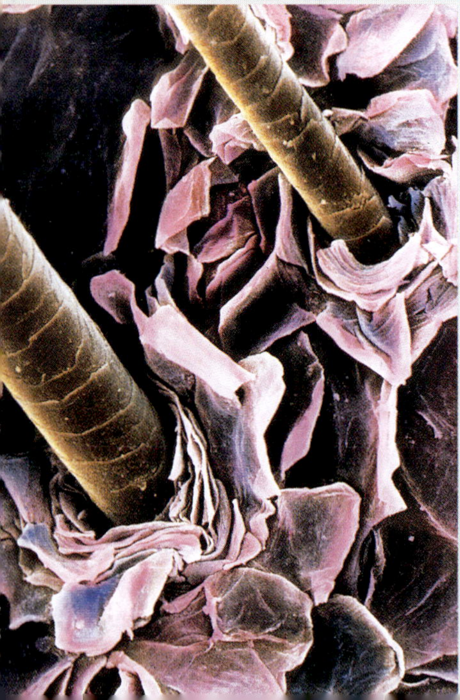

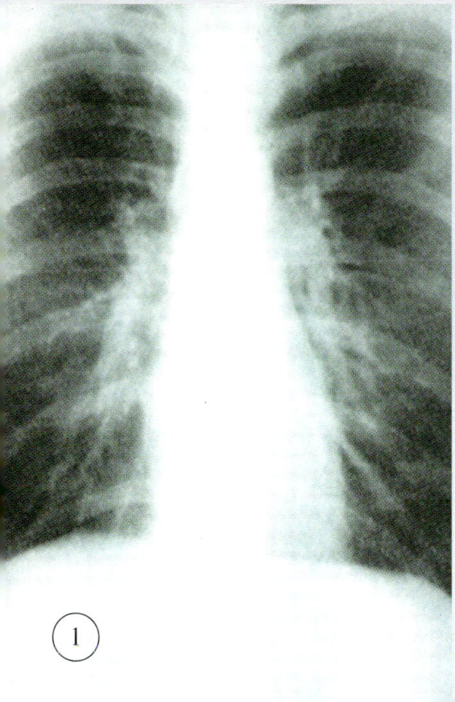

1

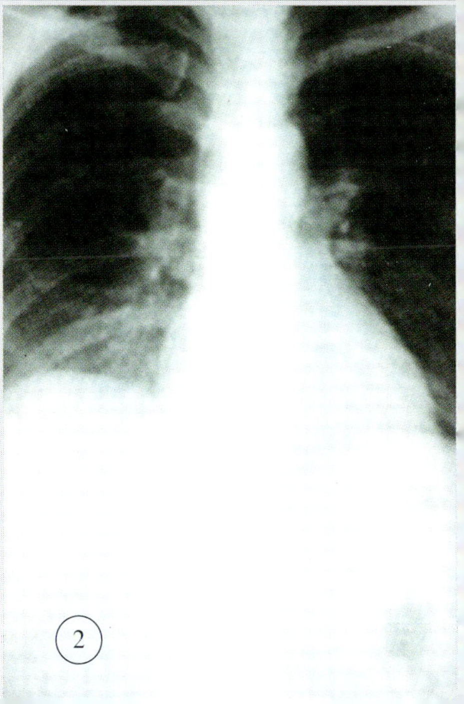

2

Picture Cards

Skin

As we grow old our skin becomes more and more wrinkled. Frequent or excessive exposure to the sun causes the skin to age prematurely and can also result in skin cancer.

Picture Cards

X-rays of Lungs

When we inhale, the rib cage expands and the diaphragm falls, pulling air into the lungs (left). When we exhale, the rib cage contracts and the diaphragm rises, forcing air from the lungs (right).

Picture Cards

Tattoos

Many of the world's people tattoo their bodies by injecting dye under the skin. The markings may be made to identify to which group an individual belongs or in the belief that the designs will ward off evil. Sometimes they are simply decorative.

Picture Cards

Blood Letting

Blood letting (deliberately causing a patient to bleed) was practiced by doctors up until the nineteenth century. It was thought to cleanse the blood and thereby cure illness. In reality, blood letting often left the patient weaker and sicker.

Picture Cards

Medications

Prescription medicines are carefully measured to ensure that the proper dosage is taken. It can be dangerous to take any kind of medication or drug without medical advice.

Picture Cards

The Pupil

The pupil is the dark part of the eye. In dim light, the pupil opens to let in more light. In bright light, the pupil contracts to protect the eye.

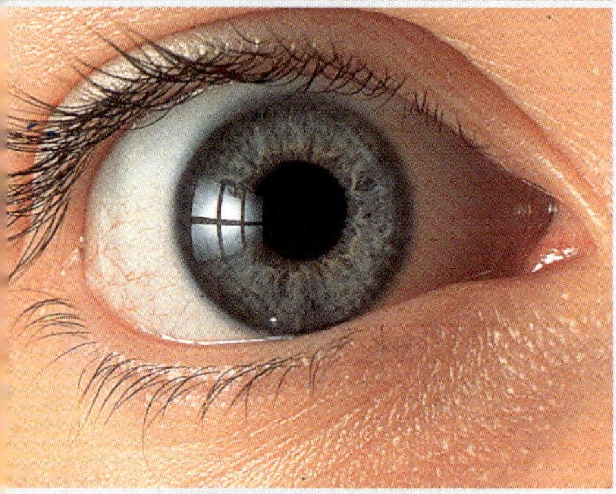
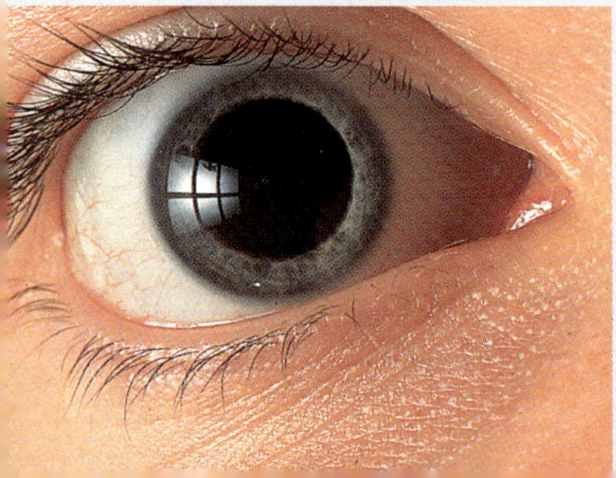
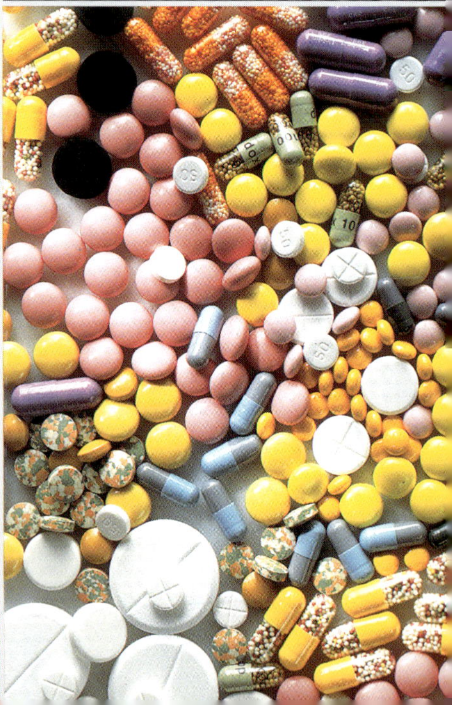

Titles in the Megascope series:

Amazing Nature

Searching for Human Origins

Understanding the Human Body

Life in the Middle Ages

Mysteries, True and False

The Pharaohs of Ancient Egypt

BARRON'S

Barron's Educational Series, Inc.
250 Wireless Blvd., Hauppauge, NY 11788